STATE PENSIONS
IN
BRITAIN

JOHN CREEDY

CAMBRIDGE UNIVERSITY PRESS

CAMBRIDGE

LONDON   NEW YORK   NEW ROCHELLE

MELBOURNE   SYDNEY

Published by the Press Syndicate of the University of Cambridge
The Pitt Building, Trumpington Street, Cambridge CB2 1RP
32 East 57th Street, New York, NY 10022, USA
296 Beaconsfield Parade, Middle Park, Melbourne 3206, Australia

© The National Institute of Economic and Social Research 1982

First published 1982

Printed in Great Britain at The Pitman Press, Bath

Library of Congress catalogue card number: 81–15507

British Library Cataloguing in Publication Data
Creedy, John
State pensions in Britain.—(Occasional papers/
The National Institute of Economic and Social
Research; 33)
1. Old age pensions—Great Britain
I. Title II. Series
368.4'3'0941   HD716.G8

ISBN 0 521 24519 2

THE NATIONAL INSTITUTE OF
ECONOMIC AND SOCIAL RESEARCH

Occasional Papers
XXXIII

STATE PENSIONS
IN BRITAIN

2 DEAN TRENCH STREET, SMITH SQUARE, LONDON, SW1P 3HE
The National Institute of Economic and Social Research is an independent, non-profit-making body, founded in 1938. It has as its aim the promotion of realistic research, particularly in the field of economics. It conducts research by its own research staff and in cooperation with the universities and other academic bodies. The results of the work done under the Institute's auspices are published in several series, and a list of its recent publications will be found at the end of this volume.

CONTENTS

TABLES

PREFACE

This book arose out of a larger project on 'Earnings and Employment Experience of Individuals', which was financed by the Department of Health and Social Security but the views expressed are the responsibility of the author alone. The book represents an attempt to present an essentially technical argument in non-technical language. It must be confessed that I have not found this to be an easy task, but hope that others beside myself may gain something from these struggles to summarise analysis without the use of mathematical notation.

I should particularly like to thank Peter Hart of the National Institute and the University of Reading for his considerable help and advice. He was the director of the project, and devoted a very large amount of time and energy to it. His careful reading of the successive drafts and his constructive criticism and encouragement have been invaluable to me. I am grateful also to the Director, Mr David Worswick, who made many helpful suggestions, and the Secretary, Mrs Kit Jones, for her encouragement and advice. Barry Thomas also made helpful comments on one of the drafts, as did participants at various universities where some of the material has been presented. I should also like to thank Michele Foot and Linda Roberts for their expert computing assistance at different stages of the project, Angela Manfield and Patricia Wears for their superb typing and Frances Robinson who prepared the study for the press.

I am also grateful to Basil Blackwell for permission to reproduce the tables and formulae in appendix B from the *Oxford Bulletin of Economics and Statistics*, vol. 42, no. 1, February 1980, to the Cambridge University Press for permission to reproduce charts 4.1 and B1 from the *Economic Journal*, vol. 89, June 1979 and to the Colston Society for their permission to reproduce charts 3.1, 3.2 and 3.4 from Colston Paper No. 31.

INTRODUCTION

SOME NATIONAL INSURANCE ISSUES

It is rather sobering to reflect that men who were born in 1911, the year the first National Insurance Act was passed, had not reached retirement age by the time the Social Security Act of 1975 was passed. Although the interval between these two landmarks in insurance and social security legislation represents less than a lifetime, the regulations and circumstances surrounding the payment of contributions and receipt of benefits have varied considerably. The same period has also seen significant changes in the age distribution of the population, in particular a large increase in the proportion of people over the age of 65 years, and large changes in labour force participation and in unemployment rates. Despite the large changes in social, economic and demographic factors which have influenced revisions to many details of particular schemes, the main issues of debate have actually remained more or less unchanged over the period. Although it is not the purpose of this study to examine all of these issues in detail, it is perhaps useful at this stage to consider some of the general problems of National Insurance. It should rapidly become clear that they are closely interrelated.

Contributions

First, there are the issues surrounding the contributory principle which has been an important feature of National Insurance since 1911, and which received its most extensive support in the famous report by Beveridge.[1] It was initially regarded as very important to draw a distinction between 'assistance' and 'insurance', in particular to avoid the stigma of the means-test as it was applied in the early years of this century. In 1911 the threshold income above which individuals paid taxes was much higher in relation to average income, so that a much smaller proportion of the population was liable to pay income tax. It was also administratively much more convenient to give an allowance irrespective of means, but in return for contributions.[2]

---

[1] *Report on Social Insurance and Allied Services*, Cmnd 6404, London, HMSO, 1942.
[2] It is interesting that A. C. Pigou in *Economics of Welfare*, London, Macmillan, 1920, in his chapter on insurance (deleted in later editions) was in favour of benefits being financed from general taxation. A useful discussion of the contributory principle can be found in A. T. Peacock, *The Economics of National Insurance*, London, William Hodge & Co., 1952.

Nevertheless the relationship between individual contributions and benefits has always been, to say the least, very tenuous. For example, benefits from the National Health services bear no relation to insurance contributions; nor do child and other dependants' benefits. Since coverage is universal and contributions are compulsory they are really equivalent to a rather special kind of tax, and are commonly regarded as such. Despite repeated arguments to the effect that the term 'insurance' is a complete misnomer, it is unfortunately still true that attachment to the insurance myth affects practical decisions and leads to confused thinking.[1] Some of the problems which arise through attachment to an insurance myth in the context of schemes for retirement pensions will be considered in this book.

It is worth stressing here that a National Insurance system, which relies on special contributions and where benefits can be exhausted, can never completely replace a means-tested system, since there will always be some individuals who are ineligible for National Insurance benefits for a variety of reasons. Under the system operating in Britain such means-tested benefits are known as Supplementary Benefits which are payable to people not in full-time work. In the original design of the National Insurance system it was of course envisaged that the role of Supplementary Benefits (or of National Assistance, as it was previously called) would be much reduced. Indeed, it has been noted that the insurance system arose directly out of the failure of the previous system of poor relief to cope with the situation, and a desire to improve administrative efficiency, and to avoid the problems usually associated with means-tested systems (such as stigma and the low take-up of benefits). It is also well known that Beveridge strongly argued that the successful operation of his system depended on a commitment by the state to full employment, and required levels of benefits which were adequate for conventional needs. However, simultaneous operation of the National Insurance and Supplementary Benefit systems has for many years been less than perfect, and the work of the latter system has increased substantially in recent years. For many years the means-tested benefits, for unemployment and for pensions, have exceeded the corresponding insurance benefits, although the official reasons for these anomalies have not usually been made clear. The role of the Supplementary Benefit system will not be examined in this book, however.

Benefits

Whatever the principles affecting policy decisions, whether they are

---

[1] For example, see T. Wilson (ed.), *Pensions, Inflation and Growth*, London, Heinemann, 1974, p. 17. The issue of the relationship between contributions and income taxation is discussed later in this book, in chapter 7 and in appendix C.

influenced by pseudo-insurance principles or by explicit analysis of a tax-transfer system, the formidable problem remains of setting the appropriate levels of benefits and taxes.[1] As this study is concerned with state pensions only, and not with the rest of the system of personal taxation, it seems most appropriate to continue the usual practice of referring to rates of contributions rather than to rates of taxes.

Now benefits and contributions were initially set at a flat rate per week, and this is administratively the simplest kind of scheme to operate and requires least information. At an early stage the system of flat-rate contributions was criticised for being regressive, as contributions formed a higher proportion of weekly income for the lower than for the higher income earners. But the question of the regressivity or otherwise of such a system is much more complex, since, for example, many high earners would in practice never have occasion to draw unemployment benefits at all, and pensions are not closely related to the timing of contributions.

The change towards earnings-related schemes, accelerated in the 1960s and completed by the 1975 Act, has very important consequences for the feasible levels of benefits which can be financed from contributions. For example, if the total amount of revenue available for distribution in benefits remains unchanged, then the introduction of earnings-related benefits to certain high earners necessarily implies that the basic minimum level of benefits must be reduced. There is therefore a clear trade-off between the desire to maintain high replacement rates (roughly defined as the ratio of benefits to income while in work) and the desire to maintain an adequate minimum benefit. An obvious policy alternative would be to raise the level of contributions. The precise nature of the trade-offs involved, and their implications for income redistribution, have not previously been specified in detail. A main feature of the present study is therefore the examination of the range of feasible policy alternatives concerning rates of contributions and benefits in different types of pension system. The implications for redistribution of each alternative system are also examined. It is argued that detailed information of this kind is necessary for rational discussion of policy, and that the implications of previous policy decisions have not always been fully understood.

For example, it can be argued that the case in favour of earnings-related schemes has not been made clear, and is often framed in pseudo-insurance terms combined with vague arguments relating to

---

[1] It seems that the task of preparing estimates of contributions appropriate to benefits proposed for the 1911 National Insurance Act fell to Alfred Flux. His comment some years later is rather an understatement, 'The basis of ascertained fact upon which it was necessary to build at that time was by no means as broad or as solid as could have been desired' (see *Journal of the Royal Statistical Society*, A, 1934, p. 105).

taxable capacity. Thus, it has been suggested that earnings-related contributions will only willingly be paid in return for earnings-related pensions. Some of these arguments will therefore be considered in this study.

As far as costs of administration are concerned, it is clear that a scheme based on earnings-related benefits is much more expensive than one based on flat-rate benefits, since a continuous record of earnings has to be maintained. The data handling problems are clearly considerable and expensive to overcome.[1] Earnings-related contributions which are deducted from gross earnings along with PAYE income taxation are of course no more expensive to collect than flat-rate contributions. A detailed examination of the administrative costs of alternative schemes is not, however, included in this study although they would provide a useful subject of investigation.

Incentives

All systems of income maintenance, from at least the Elizabethan Poor Laws, have been very concerned with the issue of what is referred to in insurance terms as moral hazard. For example, the system must ensure that all recipients of unemployment benefit are genuinely involuntarily unemployed and are actively seeking employment. The problem is obviously less important in the context of old age pensions, where falsification of age would be required. But the ambivalence of the legislation can be seen in the coexistence of pseudo-insurance features with an earnings rule for pensions, whereby the pension is reduced for those receiving an income above a specified limit, irrespective of the history of contributions.[2]

There is, however, the possibility that the imposition of a particular system of insurance contributions, and the promise of any given pension during retirement, may affect the labour supply of some individuals. Even if early retirement is not allowed, there may be changes in savings and labour supply behaviour over working life. It is, however, fair to say that there has been very little progress in measuring such responses. In common with the majority of studies of tax-transfer systems, this book abstracts from possible induced changes in the distribution of earnings which may result from a change in the tax structure. In the case of pension schemes it may be suggested that any effect on age-earnings profiles of a change in pensions is likely to take place very slowly; indeed,

---

[1] For a staggering description of the operations of the central office of the Department of Health and Social Security at Newcastle in the early 1970s see *Report of the Committee on Abuse of Social Security Benefits*, Cmnd 5228, London, HMSO, 1973, pp. 7–8.
[2] But until 1980, those who retired early with an occupational pension could draw unemployment benefit for twelve months.

age-earnings profiles have shown surprising stability in the face of very large structural changes in the economy. Furthermore, it will be seen that the contrasts between different schemes are so large that it may be argued that comparisons will be robust. To the extent that earnings are endogenous the results may be interpreted as showing the limits to redistribution.

National Insurance finance

There remain the issues associated with the finance of benefits. Now in practice National Insurance payments cannot be financed solely from a fund into which contributions are paid and which accumulates at compound interest. This is obviously the case in systems where virtually no risk rating is used and where benefits are adjusted for inflation and productivity growth. With unemployment benefits in particular, the total amount needed at any time depends crucially on the state of the economy as a whole, which is also affected by circumstances in world markets. While a fund may not always be adequate (as, for example, in the inter-war years) it also seems unreasonable to finance each year's benefits solely from the contributions and taxes of the same year. This would make continuity in the real levels of benefits impossible to achieve, and the burden of taxation would place considerable strain on the 'social contracts' required to sustain any agreed scheme. Furthermore, in the case of pensions it can be argued that contributions should to some extent represent genuine savings (involving the deferment of consumption), and should help to finance investment and contribute to the real growth of the economy.

The British system contains only a partial fund, and is financed mainly on a pay-as-you-go basis. Unfortunately, the system has the curious and inconsistent feature whereby contributions are largely equivalent to an earmarked tax, but since 1976 there has been a tax surcharge on employers' contributions which goes directly to central exchequer funds. Some further discussion of the finance of benefits is therefore provided later in this book.

A LIFETIME PERSPECTIVE

At this stage it is necessary to stress an underlying feature of this study: the lifetime perspective. Pension schemes provide a clear and obvious example of an arrangement for redistributing some of each individual's income between working life and retirement.[1] In examining alternative

[1] Similarly, individuals may experience unemployment at a number of stages over their working life, and it is evident that some people are very prone to unemployment, while others never experience a single spell of unemployment.

schemes for the administration of pensions, it therefore makes little sense to examine the position of a cross-section of individuals at one point in time. It is very difficult to interpret 'redistribution between individuals' in the context of pension schemes unless this refers to some measure of the lifetime incomes of a group of people who were born in the same year and whose working and retired lives therefore cover comparable periods in terms of labour market conditions and real levels of contributions and benefits.

It should, however, be stated that there are many difficult problems associated with defining (not to mention measuring) lifetime earnings and their redistribution. Many of these problems, for example the question of how to treat differences in length of life in measuring the dispersion of lifetime earnings, cannot be examined here. In particular it should be stressed that no attempt has been made to measure the inequality of earnings, but rather to describe the pattern of changes over life. The statistical measures of dispersion used have been chosen for pragmatic reasons, especially for their analytical tractability.

PLAN OF THE BOOK

It is necessary to stress at this stage that the scope of the present book is rather limited. Indeed there are many interesting and important issues which are not discussed at all. For example, there is no attempt to examine the complexities of the private pension industry, and the management of private pension funds. These funds have grown significantly in recent years, and they warrant separate and extensive treatment.

The analysis contained in this book relates to individual male income recipients, and takes no account of the effects of household size or of marital status on pensions. There are various benefits for dependants and widows, and it is clear that they should affect considerations of state pension finance and of the extent of redistribution implied by the scheme. The present analysis is limited not only to individuals (rather than households), but to a single cohort; that is, a group of individuals all of whom were born in the same year. In a complete analysis of pensions a considerable amount of energy would have to be devoted to the study of demographic factors. Forecasts of population growth and structure are obviously crucial.

Furthermore, there is no attempt to examine separate occupations; the earnings distributions used refer to all occupations combined. But the analysis is also limited to individuals who are assumed to be eligible for full pension benefits on retirement; that is, it considers individuals who have fairly stable employment histories and have not spent a significant proportion of their life either unemployed, or sick, or completely out of the labour force. A comprehensive analysis would need to consider the extent to which individuals who have suffered large amounts of sickness and unemployment during working life, but have nevertheless paid a substantial amount of National Insurance contributions, must rely on Supplementary Benefits in retirement.

The main objective of this partial analysis of pension schemes is to examine a number of related aspects of pensions which seem to have been given relatively little attention in the past. While these issues represent only part of a complete analysis of pensions, it is nevertheless suggested that they are of importance, and warrant close consideration. The particular subjects covered in the present study are all related to aspects of the new state scheme which was introduced in Britain in April 1978. The details of this new scheme are set out in chapter 2, which also provides further information about the plan of this book and introduces the terminology used to describe the various schemes which are examined in later chapters.

It has been noted that the Social Security Act of 1975 finalised the movement in Britain towards earnings-related insurance benefits and contributions (although subsequent legislation in 1980 aimed to abolish earnings-related unemployment benefit). While it is obvious that this must involve either a reduction in the basic minimum pension or an increase in the rate of contributions, the precise nature of the trade-offs involved are not usually made explicit. The purpose of chapter 3 is to examine the relationship between feasible pension levels and contribution rates, in a number of alternative state schemes. This chapter shows the extent to which the objective of reducing poverty in old age through state pensions must be sacrificed in any attempt to increase the extent of income replacement during retirement.

Chapter 4 then presents a simulation analysis, for a particular cohort of males, of the effects on pension costs of basing the earnings-related component of the two-tier pension on an average of earnings in the individual's best twenty years (rather than on an average of earnings in all years, or in the last few years of working life). The simulations also allow for differential mortality, since it is obvious that pension costs depend on the extent to which those with relatively high pensions live longer than those with lower pensions.[1]

Chapter 5 then considers the extent to which different types of state pension scheme may redistribute income between individuals within a cohort. Since pensions necessarily involve the redistribution of some of an individual's income from working to retired life, it is necessary to

---

[1]In practice an individual's longevity may of course depend on the pension he receives, as well as his earnings during working life; but the former influence has not been examined here.

examine the redistribution of *lifetime* income, as already explained on page 6 above. The analysis of chapter 5 takes two forms. First, redistribution in alternative schemes is examined in an abstract model which does not allow for, among other things, differential mortality. These results may be taken to indicate the limits of *ex ante* redistribution implied by each of the schemes considered. Secondly, the pension simulations of chapter 4 are used to examine the extent of systematic redistribution within a single cohort. The simulations allow for earnings mobility and differential mortality, and may be regarded as indicating the extent of *ex post* redistribution. These latter results help to qualify those obtained from the more abstract model.

An important element of the new British scheme, outlined in more detail in the following chapter, is the ability to contract out of the earnings-related component of the pension, provided that a number of conditions are met. Chapter 6 examines this aspect of the scheme, and in particular it considers the individual incentives to contract out, and the method required to ensure that not all individuals leave the state scheme. These issues are considered in the context of a scheme which is similar to the new British scheme in many respects, and in the context of an alternative system which allows full contracting out of a flat-rate pension. The chapter first examines the implications of contracting out for the relationships between pensions and contributions which were discussed in chapter 3 and then shows how the results of chapter 5 (relating to redistribution) are affected by contracting out.

It has already been noted that National Insurance contributions are widely regarded as a form of income taxation, and bear virtually no relation to an insurance scheme. However, the principles on which income taxation and insurance contributions are levied are quite different, so that integration of the two systems (which has often been suggested) presents a number of complexities. Some of these problems are discussed briefly in chapter 7, which also draws together some of the results of the earlier chapters.

Finally, many of the problems examined in this book necessarily demand the use of a certain amount of mathematics and of statistics (especially elementary distribution theory). However, the discussion in the text uses only charts and tables in order to present the main results as succinctly as possible without the use of mathematical notation. Further details of the analyses and of the techniques used to obtain results are provided in three appendices. These present the basic model of pensions which is used in chapters 3, 5 and 6 (appendix A), the simulation model used in chapters 4 and 5 (appendix B), and the treatment of income taxation and National Insurance contributions used in chapter 7 (appendix C).

PENSION SCHEMES: SOME ISSUES

As explained in the previous chapter, the main analyses of state pension schemes are contained in chapters 3, 4, 5 and 6. The purpose of this chapter is to discuss some general features of pensions which are relevant for these subsequent analyses. It is not attempted to provide a comprehensive discussion of all aspects of either the welfare economics of pensions, or of the administrative problems faced by governments, since such discussions are easily available elsewhere. The first section outlines the main features of the state scheme which came into operation in April 1978. The second section then briefly discusses some aspects of pension administration, and considers the use of the term 'National Insurance' in this context. Since later chapters of this book compare alternative types of state pension scheme, the third section provides a description of the main schemes to be examined. Where subsequent chapters refer to a scheme using a brief title, reference may again be made to this section for further details.

The government pension scheme which was introduced in April 1978 may with some justification be regarded as the major innovation in social policy for many years. The scheme, under the 1975 Social Security Pensions Act, has the novel distinction of being supported in Parliament by all major political parties, though it will be interesting to observe the extent to which this agreement affects its longevity. The Social Security Act was in fact the culmination of a large amount of activity in pension planning; indeed the six years 1969–74 saw the publication of no less than three White Papers on the subject.[1]

It is difficult to know the extent to which this interest was a reflection of the increasing voting power of pensioners in an ageing population, as is sometimes suggested. Certainly the 1970s saw a revival of interest in the problems of poverty and inequality, and a realisation of the fact that

---

[1] These were, *National Superannuation and Social Insurance*, Cmnd 3883, London, HMSO, 1969; *Strategy for Pensions*, Cmnd 4755, London, HMSO, 1971; *Better Pensions (Fully protected against inflation): Proposals for a New Pensions Scheme*, Cmnd 5713, London, HMSO, 1974. Also of interest for the 1975 Act are *Explanatory Memorandum on the Social Security Pensions Bill 1975*, Cmnd 5929, London, HMSO, 1975; and *Social Security Pensions Bill 1975, Report by the Government Actuary on the Financial Provisions of the Bill*, Cmnd 5928, London, HMSO, 1975.

the aged constitute a large proportion of the poor.[1] Other important features which may be noted here include the unprecedented high rates of inflation experienced over the period, with obvious implications for those living on a fixed money income with a rapidly declining value of savings, and the fact that many of those who retired during the late 1960s and 1970s had their working lives (and therefore their ability to accumulate wealth) seriously interrupted by two world wars.

This recent activity contrasts with the very slow initial development of pensions schemes in Great Britain. The introduction of old age pensions did not take place until 1908, when their level was set at five shillings a week at 70 years of age, when other sources of income were not more than eight shillings a week. It was not until 1925 that an extension to the National Insurance scheme allowed male contributors to draw pensions from the age of 65 years.[2] The state pension was of course introduced in an attempt to deal with the growing problem of poverty in old age and, as noted above, the relief of poverty has always been stated as an objective of government pensions.

Despite their obvious importance and the energy which has been devoted to their preparation, the implications of particular pension plans have not always been generally understood.[3] This is especially true of the new state scheme which contains a large number of very novel elements, and the problems of predicting the possible financial and redistributive implications are obviously formidable.

THE NEW SCHEME INTRODUCED IN APRIL 1978

The main features of the new state scheme may be listed as follows.

---

[1] One reflection of this interest was the setting up of the Royal Commission on the Distribution of Income and Wealth. The high incidence of poverty among the aged was also important for early schemes. There had been a *Report of the Royal Commission on the Aged Poor* (under the chairmanship of Lord Aberdare) in 1907, although the commission was appointed in 1893.

[2] The process towards the passing of the 1908 Old Age Pensions Act is described vividly by F. H. Stead, *How Old Age Pensions Began to Be*, London, Methuen & Co., 1909. The principles of the 1911 Act are described in detail by L. G. Chiozza Money, *Insurance versus Poverty*, London, Methuen & Co., 1912. Before the 1925 extension there had been a *Report on the Departmental Committee on Old Age Pensions*, Cmd 410, London, HMSO, 1919.

[3] For example, C. F. Bastable, in *Public Finance*, London, Macmillan, 1903, p. 30, argued that an old age pension 'would involve a grave disturbance in financial equilibrium, which could only be restored by a series of retrograde measures in respect of taxation'. However, a useful discussion of the Labour Party's proposals, *National Superannuation. Labour's Policy for Security in Old Age*, Transport House, 1957, can be found in J. Black, 'A note on the economics of national superannuation', *Economic Journal*, vol. 68, June 1958. For discussion of later schemes see R. Titmuss, *Social Policy, an introduction*, London, Allen & Unwin, 1975, pp. 102–20; and Wilson (ed.) *Pensions, Inflation and Growth*.

Benefits

The pension is made up of two separate components or tiers. First, a flat-rate pension is paid to all eligible individuals irrespective of their earnings. Secondly, an earnings-related pension or second tier is paid, based on the length of time during which individuals have contributed to the scheme. The value of the earnings-related component cannot exceed a maximum or upper limit. For individuals who have contributed to the scheme for at least twenty years the earnings-related pension is one quarter of the difference between the individual's value of pensionable earnings (up to the limit) and the basic minimum flat-rate pension. Otherwise it is one eightieth of this difference for each year's contributions.

If, for illustrative purposes, the basic pension is assumed to be £20 per week and the upper limit £140 per week, then the pension corresponding to any value of pensionable earnings may easily be obtained. All individuals with pensionable earnings greater than or equal to £140 per week would receive a pension of £50 per week, obtained as £20 + £(140–20)/4. Those with pensionable earnings of £100 per week receive a pension of £40, calculated as £20 + £(100–20)/4. Similarly those with earnings of £60 receive a pension of £30, calculated as £20 + £(60–20)/4. It can therefore also be seen that the ratio of the pension to the value of earnings, the replacement rate, increases from an approximated 0·33 to 0·4, and then to 0·5, as earnings decrease from £140 to £100, and then to £60. This characteristic of the two-tier system, that replacement rates decline as earnings increase, has often been used to suggest that the new state scheme involves a substantial amount of income redistribution from rich to poor. However, the extent of redistribution cannot be assessed using only the benefit formula, as will be shown in some detail in chapter 5 of the present study.

Pensionable earnings

The earnings-related component or second tier in the mature scheme is based on the individual's average earnings in the best twenty years of working life, after each year's earnings have been adjusted using an index of average earnings. It is obvious that the average earnings of a number of best years must exceed the average earnings of all years, since the lowest values are excluded. Furthermore, the extent to which the two averages differ must depend on the degree to which earnings fluctuate over the individual's working life. However, it is not until 1999 that individuals retiring can have more than twenty years relevant earnings from which to choose the best twenty, and in making detailed estimates for the first thirty years of the new scheme the Government Actuary did not explain the growing importance of this factor in later years. For this reason its effect when the scheme is fully mature is considered in some detail in chapter 4 of this study.

Contributions

Contributions are directly proportional to earnings up to a maximum weekly value, or upper limit, which is the same as that determining the maximum earnings-related pension. In the new state scheme the upper limit to earnings on which contributions must be paid is approximately seven times the basic minimum pension. Contributions are not compulsory if weekly earnings are less than the basic minimum weekly pension.

There is also an employer's contribution which is directly related to earnings up to the same limit. The fact that there is an upper limit to contributions obviously implies that the total value of contributions available for redistribution in pensions is less than if contributions were levied on the whole of earnings (using the same *rate* of contributions, of course). This aspect of the scheme is examined in chapters 3 and 4 of this study.

It is also important to note that contributions are based on gross earnings; that is, earnings before any allowances have been deducted. Furthermore, National Insurance contributions are *not* included in the usual set of allowances which may be offset against earnings for income tax purposes, so that income tax is actually levied on the contributions! These significant differences between insurance and taxation raise problems when considering proposals to integrate the two systems, and are discussed further in chapter 7.

Inflation adjustment

The basic pension and the upper limit will be adjusted at least in line with the cost of living, using a retail price index. It was however initially envisaged that the limits would be adjusted using either a price or a wage index, whichever turned out to be the larger. The method of inflation adjustment is examined briefly in chapter 5, in the context of the simulation analysis.

Contracting out

Employees who are members of certain occupational pension schemes can be contracted out of the earnings-related part of the state scheme. Those who are contracted out will continue to receive the basic or flat-rate pension, and must pay contributions to the government scheme at a lower rate than those who are full members. The system is therefore one of partial contracting out. The ability to contract out of the British state pension scheme is another of its very novel elements, and of course it was not possible to know in advance how many employees would in fact contract out. The nature of the incentives to contract out, and its implications for those who remain in the state scheme, are therefore examined in some detail in chapter 6. This aspect of the new scheme has had a substantial impact on the private pension industry, but this is outside the scope of the present study.

The 1975 Social Security Pensions Act contains other provisions; in particular relating to job mobility and to working women (who are now treated in the same way as men, except that they receive their pensions from age 60 years), and to widows (who will be given their husbands' full pension rights if they are widowed over 50 years of age, or at any age when they support a young family). But the points discussed under the five headings above are the main innovations with which this study is concerned.

ADMINISTRATION OF PENSIONS

There are basically two polar methods of operating pension schemes: the 'funded' and the 'pay-as-you-go' scheme. However, in practice very few schemes adhere rigidly to either method.

Funded schemes

In a fully funded pension scheme all contributions are effectively deposited into a fund, which accumulates at compound interest. All benefits are paid from the fund, which must be of sufficient size to cover all expected future commitments. It is usually argued that this kind of system is most suitable for a private pension scheme, since the existence of a fund ensures that liabilities could be met in the event of bankruptcy of the firm or group providing the pensions. The fund may be administered on a risk pooling basis, for a group of individuals who are thought to face similar kinds of risks (for example, those in a certain occupation), and the scheme may have an explicit degree of income redistribution built into it. All individuals may not therefore expect the same rate of return from their contributions, although the system as a whole must be self-financed. Alternatively the fund may be an actuarial fund, in which case each individual's contributions and benefits are determined after a process of screening in order to assess the individual's risks relating to earnings variations and life expectancy. In this case all members of the fund have the same expected (or *ex ante*) rate of return from the scheme. Any *ex post* redistribution would ideally arise only through purely random variations in earnings and age at death, and would not be systematically related to earnings. In each case the size of the required fund will also depend on the anticipated number of deaths before retirement, and the extent of other 'lost' benefits, perhaps caused by mobility (though the new scheme allows rights to be retained).

Pay-as-you-go schemes

Turning to the operating of pay-as-you-go schemes, their rigorous application would involve the complete absence of a fund, and pensions and contributions would be adjusted regularly according to demographic changes, growth or inflation. In practice, as in the new state scheme, a partial fund is often accumulated and contributions may include a donation from central exchequer funds as well as some of the revenue from contributions. It is often argued that the successful operation of a pay-as-you-go scheme requires a social contract between three generations, since the support of the retired population by the active labour force will only be continued on the understanding that the next generation of workers will actually vote to continue the scheme. The analysis of such a scheme clearly requires detailed forecasts of demographic and many other trends.

State pensions and insurance schemes

Many discussions of government pension schemes adopt the term Social or National Insurance, and discuss the regulations as if they were part of an actuarially sound scheme. This terminology is, however, most unfortunate since there are many reasons why state schemes differ from an ideal insurance scheme, even when a fund is accumulated.

First, there is virtually no real risk rating in state schemes, for example by medical examinations. Secondly, since benefits are not related to the timing of contributions, they are not related to the accumulated value of contributions. Thirdly, in the new scheme contributions which are paid for more than twenty years are only relevant in so far as earnings during those years may help to increase the individual's average twenty best years' earnings. Fourthly, the benefits paid during retirement may be reduced if additional income from other sources exceeds a threshold level, irrespective of previous contributions to the scheme (this refers to the so-called earnings rule). Fifthly, benefits are higher for married men, while there is no difference between contributions of single and married individuals. Sixthly, contracted benefits should also depend on the anticipated rate of interest over the period during which contributions accumulate, and can only be fixed in nominal terms rather than in real terms. However, since pensions in the new scheme are to be adjusted for inflation, it is virtually impossible for a fund to remain actuarially sound. The fact that occupational schemes, in order to qualify as contracted out schemes, must also provide inflation-adjusted pensions, has of course meant that the state must agree to provide support to private schemes when necessary. Finally, the introduction of a new government scheme creates difficulties relating to those already retired and soon to retire, and will usually involve contributors receiving full benefits before it is actuarially sound for them to do so.

These points, which indicate the misleading nature of the term Social Insurance, and the remoteness of the state pension scheme from the operation of an actuarial fund (with individual risk rating) should not necessarily be regarded as criticisms, and may perhaps actually serve to justify the existence of some features of government pension plans. Neither do they necessarily conflict with the use of some kind of pension fund whereby pensions are paid out of an hypothecated tax. Indeed it is best to keep the discussion of insurance features of social security plans quite separate from a discussion of issues such as the integration of tax and social security contributions (involving the abolition of hypothecated payments). The latter issue will therefore be considered later in this book, in chapter 7.

The role of a state scheme

It may reasonably be argued that the appropriate functions of a state scheme are very different from those of an insurance scheme; the continued use of the term social insurance can only lead to confusion.[1] For example, a scheme which provides efficient risk rating would not provide an adequate pension for the significant proportion of the population with high risks. Furthermore, many of the risks to which individuals are subject, such as structural change, unemployment and inflation, are associated with the aggregate performance of the economy, and cannot really be identified with individual characteristics. It has been noted that in an insurance scheme with individual risk rating all redistribution should be random, whereas there may be arguments for using some of the contributions of the higher earners to pay higher pensions to those who would otherwise constitute the aged poor.

Furthermore, in terms of economic efficiency, it may be appropriate for the state to make all the relevant decisions about the amount which individuals with given incomes during their working lives will, on average, require during their retirement. The collection of all the required information, including the assessment of life expectation, and the likely future course of the economy, would be very difficult and costly (if indeed possible) for individuals and for insurance companies. This may well be left to an appropriate centralised state agency. This

[1] Useful discussions of many of the issues referred to briefly here can be found in P. A. Diamond, 'A framework for social security analysis', *Journal of Public Economics*, vol. 8, 1977, and R. Disney, 'Unemployment and National Insurance', in J. Creedy (ed.), *The Economics of Unemployment in Britain*, London, Butterworths, 1981.

argument is concerned with the efficiency of information collection and decision making, but it has also been suggested that in the absence of state pensions most individuals would save insufficient amounts to finance consumption during their retirement. This further argument for state pensions is not simply a paternalistic argument, since it may be more efficient than the provision of additional income transfer mechanisms to the aged, through, for example, a means-tested sector. The argument that individuals would not save appropriate amounts is of course notoriously difficult to test rigorously, and not surprisingly some researchers have suggested that aggregate savings are reduced by state pensions. However, these interesting issues concerning the determinants of private savings cannot be examined here.

Method of analysis

It is not of course the purpose of this study to produce the kind of estimates which might be made by the Government Actuary in providing advice about the appropriate levels of contributions and benefits. Rather, some aspects of state pension schemes, and in particular the new British pension scheme, which do not seem to have been given sufficient attention in the past, are examined. A major problem concerns the nature of the trade-offs involved in the policy choices between various types of scheme and the levels of benefits and contributions which are feasible; and the extent of redistribution in each case. For this reason it is most appropriate to examine the trade-offs in the context of funded schemes for separate generations or cohorts of individuals. Actuarial funds which operate perfectly efficient risk rating are not considered, but comparisons are made of the benefits which may be paid during retirement from the contributions of a particular cohort to an interest earning fund. Given the interest in examining trade-offs and redistribution, it makes little sense to consider pension schemes which are not self-financing, as it would then be necessary to consider the implications of the various methods used to supplement a fund. Thus only revenue neutral comparisons are appropriate. It will, however, be seen that the analysis of funded schemes provides useful information about the possibilities for pay-as-you-go schemes. Alternative plans are outlined in the following section.

ALTERNATIVE PENSION SCHEMES

This section describes in general terms the types of scheme which are compared in later chapters of this book.

Flat-rate schemes

Flat-rate schemes of contributions and benefits simply involve payments at a fixed rate irrespective of an individual's earnings. The first pension schemes in Britain paid a flat-rate pension without the need for previous contributions, but when contributions were introduced they were initially set at a fixed value per person.

Earnings-related schemes

Contributions may alternatively be calculated as a proportion of a particular measure of earnings, usually gross earnings (as in the present scheme in Britain). The proportional rate of contributions is usually constant, except that there may be an upper limit to the value of earnings on which contributions are levied. For earnings above the upper limit the marginal contributions rate (the contributions paid on an additional £1 of earnings) is therefore zero. In some systems individuals may not be liable to pay contributions until a certain threshold, or lower earnings limit, has been passed. Since contributions are based on gross earnings, not on earnings measured only from the lower limit, the marginal contributions rate is extremely high at levels of earnings equal to the lower limit.

It is therefore possible to combine earnings-related contributions (either with no earnings limits, or with upper and lower limits) with a scheme paying flat-rate pensions. This kind of scheme is in fact considered in some detail in the present book.

Alternatively, earnings-related contributions may be combined with earnings-related pensions, whereby the benefits are calculated as a proportion of some measure of earnings obtained during the individual's lifetime. The measure of pensionable earnings may, for example, be the final year's earnings, or an average of earnings over a specified number of years, or a more complex measure such as that specified in the British state scheme. The implications of using different measures of pensionable earnings are considered in this study. As with contributions, there may be an upper limit to the value of earnings on which the pension is calculated.

Two-tier pensions

If pensions were directly proportional to pensionable earnings, then of course those in poverty during their working lives would tend to remain in poverty during old age. For this reason most schemes where it is desired to have an earnings-related component to the pension are of the two-tier variety. Thus a flat-rate pension is paid to all eligible individuals, and an earnings-related second-tier is based on the difference between pensionable earnings and the flat-rate pension. Of course, the second-tier may also have an upper limit, as in the British scheme.

Policy choices

It is clear that as schemes increase in complexity there are more policy choices to be made. With flat-rate contributions and benefits only two policy variables have to be set, but of course these cannot be chosen independently since the total contributions must be sufficient to finance benefits. If earnings-related contributions are combined with flat-rate benefits there are still only two policy variables; but the introduction of a two-tier pension involves the need to decide on the proportional pension rate to be used in the upper tier. With three policy variables and the constraint that the scheme should be self-financing, it is evident that only two of the variables can be chosen independently; having set two, there are no degrees of freedom available in the choice of the third variable. Consideration of the range of feasible policy choices is therefore more complicated than when only two variables are involved.

The introduction of an upper earnings limit to both contributions and pensions obviously adds two more policy variables, so that a scheme of earnings-related contributions combined with a two-tier pension re-quires a decision to be made about the appropriate values of five policy variables, although there are only four degrees of freedom in the choices available. However, the initial decision may be made that the upper earnings limits should be the same for both contributions and benefits, thereby reducing the number of degrees of freedom in policy choices to three. The two limits are equal in the current British scheme, but there is obviously no necessary reason for this to be the case.

It is argued here that the nature of the feasible policy choices which are available in different types of state pension schemes, and the nature of the trade-offs which must be accepted, have not been fully appreciated by those responsible for planning pensions. In particular, the extent to which the introduction of an upper tier to pensions and the imposition of an upper earnings limit to contributions make the achievement of an adequate basic pension more difficult to attain seems to have been given relatively little attention. Their importance for the design of insurance and social security systems justifies their further examination here.

CONTRIBUTIONS AND BENEFITS

It is clear that even where the rules for determining any individual's contributions and subsequent pension entitlement are very simple, as in a flat-rate system, the problem of deciding on the precise numerical values presents formidable difficulties. For example, it is necessary to set the value of the basic minimum pension, which is usually specified in relation to average earnings. The range of information required for such an exercise is indeed quite staggering; it includes information about retirement behaviour, earnings and labour force participation over the life cycle and detailed demographic forecasts including rates of mortality and their relation to earnings. Moreover all these have to be combined with forecasts of the likely course of interest rates, productivity growth and the rate of increase of prices. Precise numerical assumptions about these economic variables, whether explicit or otherwise, must be made in order to produce the required calculations.

In view of this vast complexity, it is not surprising that most analyses of pensions have abstracted from many of the complicating factors, in order to focus attention on particular points of interest. As explained in the previous chapter, the main interest here is in examining the nature of the trade-offs which are relevant in making policy choices. It is necessary to know which objectives may be mutually inconsistent, for example. For this reason a framework of analysis is used which allows convenient comparisons between alternative systems to be made, but which abstracts from many elements of reality. While such complications may obviously affect the levels of contributions and benefits, it is argued that their introduction would not significantly affect comparisons between the various schemes. The previous chapter also suggested that the most appropriate comparisons were for funded schemes, since if pensions cannot be financed from contributions there are further implications for the general system of taxation which must be considered.

The main issues to be examined here are therefore quite different from those considered in earlier studies of pensions, which used a different framework of analysis. One basic method of examining the relationship between contributions and the benefits which they could finance, which was popular in earlier discussions, involves the comparison between pay-as-you-go schemes which allow the aged to share in the general

growth of real earnings, and the funded scheme in which each generation fully finances its own subsequent benefits. In these models a
constant rate of productivity growth is imposed on average earnings and
earnings-related contributions are accumulated at a fixed rate of interest
for a given number of years. With a constant rate of population growth it
is then a fairly straightforward matter to examine the benefits which
these total contributions could finance. The convenient assumption
about population growth avoids the difficulties associated with differential mortality rates and enables a simple relationship between the sizes of
the working and of the retired populations to be obtained. To make the
analysis even more tractable benefits are usually specified in terms of
their proportion to current real earnings.[1]

By concentrating on earnings-related schemes of contributions and
benefits it is only necessary to consider *average* earnings and their growth.
Similar models have also been used to examine the contribution of
pension funds, as a source of investment finance, to the rate of growth of
the economy. The question of the optimal amount of funding required in
order to secure maximum economic growth can therefore also be
considered using such a framework.

Nevertheless when it is required to examine the feasible combinations
of contributions and pensions under different kinds of pension formulae,
the models described above no longer seem to be appropriate. Thus, if a
basic minimum income has to be earned before contributions are paid
and if there is an upper limit to the amount of compulsory contributions
to a state scheme, then it is no longer possible to consider average
earnings alone and to ignore the distribution of income within the
population. A more suitable framework is therefore described in the
following section: a more formal analysis is presented in appendix A.

SOME SIMPLE COMPARISONS

A framework of analysis

Comparisons of alternative schemes and the explicit introduction of the
income distribution can unfortunately only be made at the cost of
ignoring many aspects of reality although, as argued earlier, some useful
comparisons between schemes may be made. The framework of analysis
which is used in this chapter is as follows:

---

[1] A good example is provided by H. Aaron, 'The Social Insurance paradox', *Canadian Journal of Economics*, vol. XXXII, August 1966, who states on p. 372 that 'social insurance can increase the welfare of each person if the sum of the rates of growth of population and real wages exceeds the rate of interest'.

(i) The analysis (as elsewhere in this book) is concerned only with individuals, and not with families or households.

(ii) It is concerned only with the members of a single cohort or generation of individuals. Each member of the cohort is assumed to begin work at the same age, and to retire at the same age. The framework therefore ignores differences in the length of working life. Furthermore each member of the cohort is assumed to live for the same number of years after retirement; the framework abstracts from differential mortality (which will be examined in later chapters using simulation methods). The length of retirement is of course much shorter than that of the working life.

(iii) Each individual's real earnings remain constant over working life; there are no relative movements of individuals within the distribution, so that the dispersion of earnings also remains constant. (The effects of earnings variability will be examined in later chapters using simulation methods.) It is also assumed that the distribution of gross earnings is not affected by changes in contributions or pensions, and that longevity is not affected by the level of pensions. Each individual's real pension remains unchanged over retirement.

(iv) An immediate implication of the assumption of constant earnings is that for any type of scheme (flat-rate or earnings-related), contributions remain constant over working life. Where there are earnings limits to contributions, the limits are of course also assumed to remain constant in real terms.

(v) Each individual in the cohort pays contributions into a pension fund at regular intervals, and the fund accumulates, earning interest, until the cohort retires. The total fund is then shared out among the members of the cohort, who receive a pension from the fund at regular intervals over retirement. It is assumed that the fund is exhausted in paying pensions to the cohort. There is of course no presupposition that each member obtains an equal share of the fund, or shares in direct proportion to past contributions, or earnings. The main interest of the analysis is in examining the implications of using different methods of sharing the fund.

(vi) The analysis could be carried out directly using the framework set out in (i) to (v) above. There are standard actuarial methods of deriving an expression for the accumulated value of the fund, depending on the frequency of contributions, the rate of interest, and the total length of the working period. The same methods can be used to derive an expression for the discounted value (to retirement) of pension payments, for any well specified pension formula. This would of course depend on the frequency of pension payments, the rate of interest and the length of the retirement period. The accumulated value of the fund at retirement would then need to be set equal to the discounted value of pension payments at retirement.

However, the special nature of the framework allows a further simplification to be made which allows no loss of generality. The simplification relates to the method of analysis.

Because all individuals are assumed to live to the same age, work for the same length of time, receive constant real earnings, pay constant contributions and receive a constant real pension over retirement (whatever the type of pension scheme in operation), then the analysis may proceed *as if* there were just two periods (of unequal length). The working period is consolidated into one period and retirement is consolidated into the second period. Then for each person in the cohort a single value of earnings may be used for the first working period, on which a single contribution is based. The fund, made up from the contributions of all individuals, attracts interest in the single working period. It is available for redistribution in a single pension payment to each individual in the retirement period and is obtained by multiplying the total value of contributions by what may be called an interest factor. The interest factor is equal to one (unity), plus the rate of interest attracted by the fund in the working period. The numerical value of the interest factor must of course be significantly larger than it would be if a conventional annual rate of interest were used; an appropriate numerical value, assuming a low annual real rate of interest, is about 1·6. Many of the comparisons presented below are however independent of the value of the interest factor.

It must be admitted that this last abstraction probably seems at first sight to be extremely heroic, and it is therefore necessary to stress that nothing which is essential to the analysis is being lost by making it. In particular, comparisons between alternative schemes (for example between earnings-related and flat-rate schemes) are not affected at all. To carry through the analysis with much more detail, by including the details of frequency of payment, number of years of contributions, and so on, would look more cumbersome, but the mathematical expression involving all the necessary terms would appear in precisely the same way in which what has been called the interest factor appears. Since these terms are unchanged when comparing say a two-tier scheme with a flat-rate scheme, the comparisons are unchanged by the use of this convenient simplification.

Proportional contributions and benefits

Consider first the simple earnings-related scheme for both contributions and benefits. Each individual pays a fixed proportion of his earnings during the first period into the fund, and after earning interest the resulting fund is then distributed in such a way that each individual's pension in the second period is directly proportional to his earnings obtained during the working period. The same proportional rates must apply to each individual, of course.

Thus there are two policy variables to be chosen—the two proportional rates—but there is freedom to vary only one of these independently. The need for the fund to finance the benefits fully means that a direct relationship between contributions and benefits exists. The pension rate which can be financed by contributions may be obtained as the contributions rate multiplied by what has been called the interest factor. A similar result in fact holds for the models discussed at the beginning of this section, except that the equivalent of the interest factor depends on the growth rate of income and of the population as well as the interest rate.

Now this case of proportional contributions and benefits, with no differential mortality and equal length of working lives, is really no different from a situation in which each individual saves for retirement in isolation from others, and receives the same rate of interest on his savings as every other individual. In other words if each individual can save at the same rate of interest as the pension fund, no individual gains any advantage by being a member of the fund.

Proportional contributions and flat-rate pension

If, however, the pension consists of a fixed amount which is paid to everyone irrespective of his income, then the above relationship between the proportional pension rate and the proportional contributions rate can be translated into one which refers to the flat-rate pension expressed as a proportion of average income. That is, the ratio of the flat-rate pension to average earnings must be equal to the product of the contributions rate and the interest factor. A higher contributions rate therefore increases the ratio of the basic pension to average earnings. This system implies that those with higher than average earnings obtain a lower rate of return from their contributions than do those with lower than average earnings. The latter therefore gain some advantage by being a member of the scheme, and this aspect is discussed at some length below.

Proportional contributions with a two-tier pension

A similar kind of procedure can then be used to examine the trade-off between contributions and pensions where the former are directly related to income but there is a two-tier pension. In this case all individuals receive a basic flat-rate pension irrespective of their earnings, along with a second tier which is proportional to the excess of earnings over the basic pension. Assume for the time being that there is no upper limit to the pension. Individuals with earnings during the working period of less than or equal to the basic pension therefore receive only the basic pension, while additional earnings (those above the minimum) qualify for a second-tier or proportional pension. Comparisons are no longer as simple as those above, and there is an extra policy variable or parameter in the pension formula which must be determined. It is, however, easy to see that the existence of the additional earnings-related component, or second tier, to the pension implies that in order to maintain the same basic minimum pension it will be necessary to raise the proportional rate of contributions to the fund.

The method of analysis proceeds as before. It is first necessary to know how the total value of contributions is determined, and how the total amount required to pay pensions is determined for any specified pension parameters (the flat-rate pension and the earnings-related proportion used in the second tier). The two totals are then equated, since the scheme must be self-financing, and this gives one equation to determine the feasible alternatives for three policy variables. If one variable, such as the flat-rate pension, is set at an arbitrary level it is then a simple matter to examine the alternative combinations of the other two choice variables.

Now with only a flat-rate pension the total value of pension payments is simply equal to the flat-rate pension multiplied by the number of eligible individuals. The corresponding value for the two-tier pension is, however, not so easily obtained. It is equal to the flat rate multiplied by the number of *people* with income less than or equal to the flat-rate pension, *plus* the proportional pension rate multiplied by the *total income* of those with earnings above the flat-rate pension. Further details of the necessary calculations are given in appendix A, but it can be seen that the distribution of income becomes a crucial element. However, if suitable assumptions about the income distribution are made, it is possible to calculate the value of the contributions rate required to finance any given flat-rate pension, for given values of the proportional rate used in the second tier.

The distribution of income

So far no specific assumptions about the income distribution have been made, but for more extensive comparisons some convenient assumptions are required.

It is of course necessary that the functional form or equation chosen to describe the distribution of earnings is a good approximation to reality, and is tractable within the framework used in this study. A very widely

Chart 3.1. *Distribution of earnings*

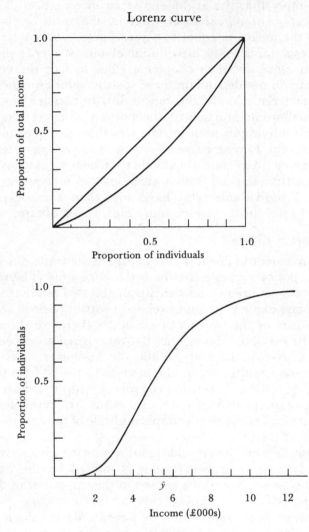

Lorenz curve

Distribution function

used form is the lognormal distribution, for which the logarithm of income follows the familiar bell-shaped normal distribution.[1] This distribution depends on two coefficients or parameters, the mean and the variance of the (natural) logarithms of income. For the present

---

[1] The standard reference work on this distribution is J. Aitchison and J. A. C. Brown, *The Lognormal Distribution; with special reference to its uses in economics*, Cambridge University Press, 1957.

calculations these are set at 8·5 and 0·2 respectively. These values of the parameters imply that the arithmetic mean income is equal to £5431, while the coefficient of variation (that is, the ratio of the standard deviation to the mean) is equal to 0·471. These values were chosen as roughly corresponding to the distribution of annual average life earnings (discussed in more detail in chapter 4), but in fact the comparisons presented here do not depend on these specific values for their interest.

Some characteristics of the theoretical distribution are shown in chart 3.1. The distribution function at the bottom of chart 3.1 shows the proportion of individuals with income less than or equal to any given amount, while the Lorenz curve shows the proportion of total income held by any given proportion of individuals. Chart 3.1 is drawn so that it is a simple matter, starting from a given level of income, to obtain the proportion of individuals who have less than that level and the proportion of total income which those individuals obtain.

A diagrammatic comparison

It is most convenient to illustrate the nature of the trade-offs involved in the choice of policy variables by the use of diagrams. The relationship between the contributions and benefits of the two alternative schemes discussed so far, namely, earnings-related contributions in combination with the flat-rate or the two-tier pension, are therefore shown in chart 3.2. The vertical axis shows the flat-rate pension expressed as a proportion of average earnings, while the horizontal axis shows the contributions rate multiplied by the interest factor. Where the pension consists only of a flat-rate pension the relationship is shown by the 45° line from the origin in chart 3.2. This is because the ratio of the pension to average earnings is equal to a simple multiple of the contributions rate and the interest factor.

The relationship for the two-tier pension scheme also turns out to be approximately a straight line, but it is shifted to the right as the proportional pension rate which is used in the upper tier of the two-tier scheme is increased. The implications for the necessary contributions rate, of a change in pensions from the flat-rate basic minimum only to the two-tier plan are therefore clearly shown in chart 3.2. The maintenance of any given basic minimum pension as a proportion of average earnings requires a much higher contributions rate as the second-tier proportional pension rate is increased. The extent of this increase may be shown by an example taken from chart 3.2. If it is required to maintain a basic minimum pension of one tenth of average earnings, the introduction of an earnings-related second tier of 20 per cent of earnings in excess of the basic pension requires an increase in the proportional contributions rate of as much as 180 per cent. Such a policy change

Chart 3.2. *Relationship between benefits and contributions*

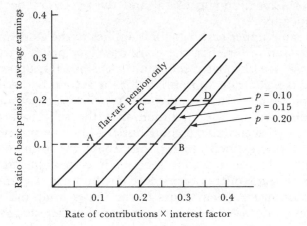

KEY
p = proportional pension rate used in the upper tier in a two-tier pension scheme

involves a shift from point A to point B along the dashed line shown in chart 3.2. The required increase is obviously lower for lower proportional pension rates, but even for a rate of 10 per cent the increase is substantial. Comparisons using a higher basic pension are shown along the dashed line CD in chart 3.2. The increase in the required contributions rate is reduced to 80 per cent where the basic minimum pension is one fifth of average earnings, but of course the absolute increase required is similar to that required for the lower basic pension.

Two-tier pension with an upper limit

The pension scheme introduced in 1978 contains a further complication in that there is an upper limit to the earnings on which contributions are paid. The same upper limit applies to pensionable earnings in the calculation of the pension. This makes the calculation of the value of total contributions required to finance any given scheme rather more awkward than for the simple proportional system, where total contributions are simply equal to the contributions rate multiplied by total income. With an upper limit the total value of contributions to the pension fund equals the contributions rate multiplied by the total income of those earning an amount not greater than the upper limit, *plus* the contributions rate multiplied by the product of the upper limit and the number of people earning more than the upper limit. These contributions, after the addition of interest, must then finance total pension payments. The value of total pensions is also complicated by the imposition of a maximum pension, and the necessary details may be found in appendix A.

Since the same upper earnings limit applies to the assessment both of contributions and of benefits, there are now four policy variables to be chosen. These are the basic minimum pension, the upper limit, the proportional pension rate appropriate for the second tier of the pension, and the proportional contributions rate. As before, a constraint on policy choices is imposed by the condition that the scheme must be self-financing; that is, accumulated contributions must be sufficient to cover all benefits. Using explicit assumptions about the form of the income distribution, as in the previous section, it is possible to derive the relationship or trade-off between the contributions rate and the basic minimum pension for given values of the upper limit and the proportional pension rate used in the upper tier. Further details are again given in appendix A. Although the basic method is the same as that applied to the pension systems without upper limits, the analysis is of course more cumbersome, and this kind of exercise could obviously produce a vast range of alternatives for consideration by the policy makers.

This range of alternatives is, however, substantially reduced by a further important constraint on the number of degrees of freedom which are available in the choice of policy variables. This constraint is imposed by the restriction in the legislation that the upper earnings limit must be approximately seven times as large as the flat-rate pension. This restriction means that in practice the upper limit is quite low relative to average earnings. Unfortunately the reasoning behind the imposition of this policy constraint has not been made very clear. It is therefore appropriate to examine alternative ratios of the upper earnings limit to the basic minimum pension and to compare this kind of system with the previous schemes shown in chart 3.2.

The comparisons may again be illustrated diagrammatically, and are shown in chart 3.3. As in chart 3.2 the vertical axis measures the basic minimum pension expressed as a proportion of average earnings, while the horizontal axis shows the product of the contributions rate and the interest factor. It can immediately be seen that when an upper limit is imposed the relationship between these variables is no longer a straight line. However, as the basic pension increases the relationship approaches the corresponding straight line in chart 3.2. For lower levels of the basic pension it is also clear that the effect of the upper limit is to increase significantly the required contributions rates, as can be seen by comparing charts 3.2 and 3.3. Moreover, chart 3.3 shows that the trade-off between the basic pension and the contributions rate is further

Chart 3.3. *Relationship between benefits and contributions* (two-tier pension with upper limit)

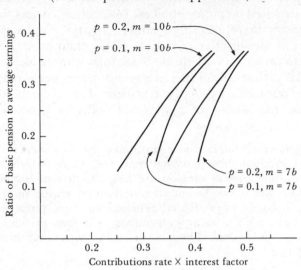

KEY
p = proportional pension rate used in upper tier
b = basic pension
m = upper earnings limit

to the right, as the ratio of the upper limit to the basic pension decreases. That is, a lower ratio requires a higher contributions rate.

SOME POLICY IMPLICATIONS

Having examined the nature of the comparisons between various schemes, some general aspects of the contrast between earnings-related and flat-rate pensions may now be considered. The analytical results presented above have shown the substantial differences between the policy trade-offs involved in the different kinds of scheme, and in particular the extent to which schemes which have an earnings-related upper tier to the pension require much higher rates of earnings-related contributions in order to maintain any given basic minimum pension. An upper limit to both contributions and pensionable earnings, as in the new government scheme which began in 1978, requires even higher rates of contributions, and of course the burden of payments is shifted towards those below the limit (this aspect, and the redistributive implications in general, are considered in chapter 5 below).

The choice between alternative pension schemes depends, of course, on the objectives of the policy makers after consideration of the constraints imposed on policy choices. In chapter 1 it was suggested that in recent years there has been much greater emphasis on income replacement as an objective of policy, rather than on schemes designed specifically to provide an adequate basic minimum pension. However, it seems unlikely that all of the decisions have been made with the appropriate trade-offs explicitly clarified. The same doubt has been expressed by the author of a detailed study of pension schemes in Europe.

How has this movement in favour of graduated pensions come about? What are the principles on which these pensions are based? Value judgements are clearly involved, and differences of opinion are likely to persist. But there is also a question of fact that has to be considered. Is there reason to believe that the social choice in favour of graduated pensions has been properly made in the sense that—whatever the value judgements—the facts of the situation have been sufficiently understood? There is reason to suspect that this condition has not been satisfied.[1]

The results of the previous section of this chapter strongly suggest that there are a number of contradictions within the present pension scheme. If it is desired to have a fairly substantial basic pension which would reduce significantly the number of old people below a given poverty standard, it is clear that a flat-rate pension combined with earnings-related contributions can achieve this objective with quite a low contributions rate. This would then provide the basis of a compulsory state pension scheme, and it would of course be left to the choice of the relatively better-off individuals to save any additional amounts for consumption in old age. Furthermore, as pointed out in chapter 2, it is the relatively low earners (those who benefit most from a higher flat-rate pension) who also suffer lack of continuity of earnings and employment. They would not therefore be able to find a suitable private scheme to cover the kind of risks which they face. Moreover, insofar as many of the risks result from cyclical unemployment or inflation and are macro-economic in nature, they could not be covered by private schemes. The opportunities for private investment of life-cycle savings for the higher earners are much greater; they may use well-established markets which operate methods of screening and risk-rating. It may therefore be argued that there is a reduced role for government intervention in this context.[2]

The argument that a universal state earnings-related scheme may be more efficient (in administration and decision making) than a collection

---

[1] See Wilson (ed.), *Pensions, Inflation and Growth*, p.22.
[2] The question of the tax treatment of contributions to private schemes cannot be considered here, although it is an important subject of study.

of private schemes has been noted in chapter 2. However, it must be stressed that this argument could not consistently be used in support of a system which also allowed contracting out, as in the British government scheme. The simultaneous operation of a state earnings-related scheme with contracting out suggests either a strong paternalistic element in the planning of the scheme, or a strong desire to stimulate the private pension industry. It has been seen that the introduction of a second tier to the pension (with or without an upper earnings limit) makes the achievement of an adequate basic pension much more difficult, so that it cannot consistently be argued that the design of the present British system reflects a desire on the part of policy makers to reduce substantially the dependence of large numbers of the aged on Supplementary Benefits.

It is, however, sometimes suggested that people would not acquiesce in the payment of contributions which are related to earnings, for the receipt of only a flat-rate pension. Nevertheless, the precise nature of this argument has not always been made clear, especially when it is realised that in a system where all pensions must be financed from contributions, exactly the same number of people may complain that they are not getting value for money in a scheme with a flat-rate pension as in a scheme with an earnings-related second tier. In particular, in both cases all those with earnings above the arithmetic mean obtain an implicit rate of return from the pension scheme which is less than the rate of interest obtained by the fund. This argument may be explained in more detail as follows.

Rates of return

The importance of the rate of interest and the interest factor has already been discussed earlier in this chapter. Now within the context of a particular state pension scheme and the simple two period model used here, each individual may easily calculate his implicit rate of return from the state scheme. It is simply equal to the ratio of his pension in the retirement period to his contribution during the working period, less one. In other words, if the ratio of the pension to the contribution is less than the interest factor appropriate for the pension fund, then the individual is receiving an implicit rate of return from the fund which is lower than the rate of interest. Alternatively, if an individual's ratio of his pension to his contributions is greater than the interest factor, then he is obtaining a higher implicit rate of return from the pension scheme than the rate of interest obtained by the aggregate fund.

In order to examine whether individuals receive value for money at different levels of earnings or in different state schemes in the present framework, which abstracts from differential mortality, it is therefore a

Chart 3.4. *Individual rates of return*

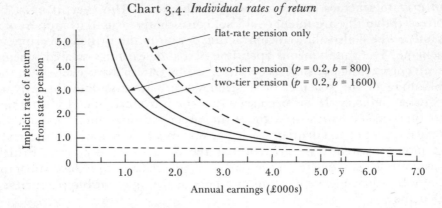

Note: The interest factor for the pension fund is 1·6
KEY
$\bar{y}$ = arithmetic mean annual earnings (£5431)
p = proportional pension for second tier
b = basic minimum pension

simple matter to compare the implicit rate of return for different earnings. Comparisons are shown in chart 3.4 between the two-tier pension and the flat-rate pension, both using proportional contributions. The examples in chart 3.4 are for an interest factor of 1·6. It can clearly be seen that those with earnings above the arithmetic mean have an implicit rate of return which is less than that obtained by the pension fund. This result applies to both flat-rate and earnings-related pension schemes. However, the effect of differential mortality, and of the tendency for the higher earners to contribute to the state scheme for a shorter length of time, would be to *raise* the rate of return of those earning more than the arithmetic mean.

The suggestion that proportional contributions must in some fundamental way be rewarded by earnings-related benefits, in order to avoid widespread protest, may perhaps be based on the implicit assumption that if a system were changed to one of flat-rate benefits, the basic rate would not be increased (or the contributions reduced) by the appropriate amount. The argument that a system with earnings-related benefits and contributions more closely resembles an actuarially sound insurance scheme has already been considered and dismissed in chapter 2.

Although it cannot therefore be maintained that *more* people would object to the flat-rate pension, it may be the case that those people (and the policy makers) are not willing to accept the greater element of redistribution which would be involved. This in turn may be based on general views about inequality and income distribution, or on views concerning the appropriateness or otherwise of a pension scheme as a device for securing redistribution. It would not, for example, be inconsistent to suggest that while more redistribution may be in some sense desirable, more efficient methods than pensions are available. Further consideration of these issues must, however, be postponed until chapter 5.

CONCLUSIONS

This chapter has examined some aspects of the relationship between contributions and pensions which are relevant when considering choices between policy alternatives. Comparisons were made of the available levels of pensions which can be financed from contributions, using a simple two-period framework which abstracts from variations in the length of working and retired lives between individuals and from variations in earnings over the working life (which are examined in detail in the next chapter). The combination of earnings-related contributions with a flat-rate pension obviously provides the highest basic pension for any given proportional contributions rate. The effect on this policy trade-off of introducing a second or upper tier to the pension was seen to be quite dramatic. These comparisons are for self-financed schemes where only the contributions are used to pay pensions to the same cohort, and there is no subsidy from general taxation or from later generations. The introduction of an upper limit to contributions and to benefits, as in the new government scheme, was also seen to require significantly higher contributions rates in order to maintain the same pension values.

The choice in favour of earnings-related pensions in Britain has meant that the value of the basic pension in the new scheme is quite low, at only about one fifth of arithmetic mean earnings. These features of the scheme seem to have been introduced in an attempt to link pensions to contributions in some way, on the argument that it would not be acceptable to give flat-rate pensions for earnings-related contributions. The upper limit may also have been introduced in order to make the system appear to look less like an income tax and to provide a further incentive for the higher earners to contract out of the state scheme, but consideration of these issues must be postponed until later in the book. It is first necessary to examine the implications of differential mortality and earnings variability over working life. Both of these factors enhance, rather than qualify, the contrasts between schemes which were made in this chapter.

SIMULATION OF PENSIONS

In order to concentrate on the differences between flat-rate and earnings-related pension schemes, in particular the extent to which the policy trade-offs differ in various schemes, it was necessary in chapter 3 to abstract from certain elements of reality. For example it was assumed that individuals face a constant earnings stream over working life, and that all live to the same age. However, the assumption of constant earnings means that the framework cannot be used to examine the implications of using alternative measures of pensionable earnings. There are of course many methods of calculating pensionable earnings, but comparison between the different methods requires explicit treatment of the variability of earnings over the life cycle.

As outlined in chapter 2 the British state scheme which began in 1978 introduced an important new element whereby earnings in only the best twenty years (after each year's earnings have been adjusted using an index of average earnings) are used in order to calculate a value of annual average earnings. The resulting average is then used as the value of pensionable earnings in order to obtain the earnings-related pension.

It is immediately obvious that the average of a selected number of best year's earnings must be higher than annual average lifetime earnings. This raises considerable difficulties for the calculation of pension costs. In order to present financial estimates for a fully mature scheme it would be necessary for the Government Actuary to have information about the expected annual average life earnings of each generation or cohort of workers, and then to have some idea of the extent to which the average of the best twenty years' earnings would be expected to exceed the lifetime average. (As mentioned above, this is unfortunately just a small component of the process of estimating financial requirements!)

In the absence of suitable data it seems that the Government Actuary first made estimates based on average earnings in the period after 1978 and then, in order to allow for selecting the best twenty years' earnings for those retiring after 1999, he made additions to the results rising from 1 per cent for those retiring in the year 2000 to 10 per cent for those retiring after 2015. His published estimates went only as far as 2018–19; for later years he said only that further contribution increases might be needed and he did not comment on the ultimate situation when the scheme would be fully mature.

The purpose of this chapter is therefore to use some information about the variation in annual earnings over the life cycle in order to examine the likely order of magnitude involved. It should first be stressed that this problem can only reasonably be examined in the context of separate cohorts of earners. Furthermore, it seems that without further information the only course of action is to carry out a simulation analysis for a particular cohort.[1] But for such an exercise to be useful it is vitally important for the simulations to be based on a well specified model which realistically describes the essential features of earnings mobility over life, and for the sensitivity of the results to the assumptions to be examined.

The next section provides comparisons of alternative measures of pensionable earnings for a particular cohort, where the variability of earnings over the working life is explicitly considered. It is followed by an examination of the extent to which total pension costs are different when alternative measures are used.

EFFECTS OF SELECTING A NUMBER OF BEST YEARS

The variation in earnings over life

The simulations reported here are based on a model which describes both the general movement of average earnings over working life and, of crucial importance in this context, the extent to which individual's earnings fluctuate from year to year. The coefficients or parameters of the model have been estimated using samples of longitudinal data which relate to male employees, and which are held by the Department of Health and Social Security. These data are described in appendix B, which also describes the simulation model in more detail. The model refers to a cohort of individuals born in 1943, and the values of earnings are in constant 1973 prices, that year being the last for which earnings data were available. The model used to generate the simulated earnings is specified in terms of the growth of real earnings for the cohort. During the period for which observations are available, the rate of growth of average earnings (over all age groups) exceeded that of prices by about 2 per cent per year, and the present simulations assume that real earnings continue to grow at this rate over the life of the cohort, in addition to the systematic changes associated with ageing alone. Now if average earnings grow faster than prices, it is clear that the upper

[1] The problem cannot of course be analysed explicitly, even with a well specified model of changes in earnings from year to year, since it is required to rank earnings from highest to lowest.

earnings limit, if adjusted using only a price index, will become unrealistically low (and this point is discussed in more detail later in this chapter). A general two-tier scheme may reasonably use an earnings index to adjust both earnings and the limits, or may base pensionable earnings on real earnings while using an earnings index to adjust the limits. But if the limits are adjusted in line with prices while there is general growth in real earnings, the earnings-related aspect of the scheme soon becomes eroded. These problems significantly complicate the analysis of the new government scheme. Indeed, its complexity alone is a serious fault; planning by individuals and by governments can be made with only a vague idea of the implications of any decision.

For present purposes it was decided to examine a two-tier scheme where pensionable earnings are based on average real earnings in the best twenty years, and where the earnings limits are set in real terms by comparison with the earnings of the cohort in the year of retirement. The use of an earnings index, as in the legislation, would imply that earnings in the earlier years of working life would be given more weight than here. Since average earnings within the cohort increase during earlier years, the effect would be to make some of these years more relevant when considering selective averaging, but the value of annual average earnings would also be increased. The difference, on average, between individuals' average best twenty years' earnings and the annual average lifetime earnings will also depend on the precise time profile of the overall growth of real earnings, and the way in which the earnings limits for the particular cohort are set. However, on balance it is worth noting that the effects of selective averaging are probably lower for schemes using an earnings index than for the present model which uses real earnings throughout. Nevertheless the general implications for two-tier systems using selective averaging would not differ significantly from those discussed here.[1]

It is also important to note that the earnings model was estimated using samples of males who had paid at least 48 National Insurance contributions in each of the years for which data were available. They therefore represent the men who were 'fully employed and almost fully employed' over the period to which the data refer.[2] Most of this group

---

[1] These statements are supported by a further analysis reported in J. Creedy, 'The British State Pension: Contributions, Benefits and Indexation', *University of Durham Working Paper in Economics*, 43, 1981. Using alternative assumptions about the general growth of earnings relative to prices, and using an earnings index, the 'twenty best years' rule gave average pensionable earnings which were about 20 per cent greater than average lifetime earnings. But the implications for total costs (shown in table 4.2 below) and for redistribution (chapter 5 below) were unchanged.

[2] During this period eligibility for National Insurance depended on the number of flat-rate contributions paid. Under the regulations of the 1975 Social Security Act, eligibility now depends on the value of earnings-related contributions paid.

are likely to be eligible for full pension benefits on retirement. The inclusion of those who experience significant and repeated unemployment would increase both the dispersion of earnings at any time and the variability of earnings from year to year. But in order to include these people in the analysis it would be necessary to consider the problems raised by eligibility requirements, and this would obviously complicate the simulation model considerably.

It is worth noting here that in the White Papers and other explanatory literature, the resulting annual average value of pensionable earnings is transformed into a weekly average in order to compare weekly pensions with weekly contributions. However, the following discussion is in terms of annual values because insufficient information about week-to-week variations in earnings is available. But this does raise the interesting question of the appropriate accounting period, since contributions are actually based on weekly earnings with no facility for annual cumulation, as in the current income tax system. The upper limit on contributions is therefore advantageous to those who experience weekly variations in earnings which cause them to cross the limit.[1]

The earnings of a simulated sample of 300 individuals during the ages of 20 to 65 years were obtained, and these form the basis of the comparisons which are presented here. Some idea of the general pattern of the age-earnings profile can be obtained from chart 4.1 which shows the smooth profiles of several measures of relative positions in the annual earnings distributions as age increases. It is, however, important to stress that individuals are *not* actually assumed to move along the profiles of chart 4.1 but experience a much less regular growth of earnings. The assumed pattern of year-to-year changes in earnings which has been used in the simulations is based on observed changes experienced by individuals over several consecutive years, and the precise details may be obtained from appendix B.

Alternative measures of earnings

The simulated earnings of the cohort were then used to obtain distributions of a number of alternative measures of pensionable earnings. Thus for each individual the earnings in each year from age 20 to 65 (in constant 1973 prices) were arranged in rank order. It was then a relatively simple matter to obtain, for each individual, the average of his earnings over the whole of the period or the average of his best ten or twenty years' earnings. For each type of average a distribution across

---

[1] There is in fact a wide variety of time periods used in the administration of the social security system. The extent to which this causes difficulties is affected largely by the extent to which effective marginal tax rates vary. For discussion of this point in relation to income tax see J. Creedy, 'Income averaging and progressive taxation', *Journal of Public Economics*, vol. 12, 1979.

Chart 4.1. *Age-earnings profiles*

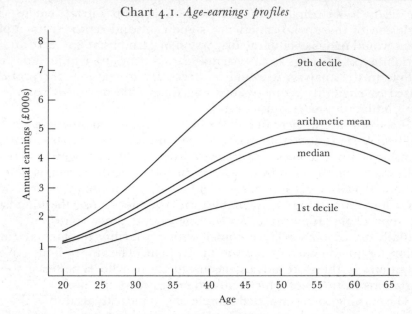

Note: 10 per cent of individuals have earnings less than or equal to the 1st decile.
20 per cent of individuals have earnings less than or equal to the 2nd decile.
50 per cent of individuals have earnings less than or equal to the median.

individuals was obtained, and the arithmetic mean values of six such distributions are compared in table 4.1. As mentioned above, these results apply to a simulated cohort born in 1943. Now for younger cohorts it is to be expected that these averages would be higher than for older cohorts. However, there is less evidence of any tendency for the variability of earnings from one year to the next to differ between cohorts.[1] The interest here is of course in examining the extent to which alternative measures of pensionable earnings differ from each other, and these differences will depend on the pattern of changes in earnings from one year to the next over the life cycle. Thus, the limitation of the simulation to a single cohort need not be regarded as particularly restrictive.

Table 4.1 shows clearly the large differences between the arithmetic mean of the distribution of annual average lifetime earnings and that of

[1] For evidence relating to this point see J. Creedy and P. E. Hart, 'Age and the distribution of earnings', *Economic Journal*, vol. 89, 1979, and J. Creedy, P. E. Hart and A. Klevmarken, 'Income mobility in Great Britain and Sweden', in A. Klevmarken and J. A. Lybeck (eds.), *The Statics and Dynamics of Earnings*, Bristol, Tieto, 1981.

Table 4.1. *Arithmetic means of alternative distributions*

Distribution	Arithmetic mean £s
Final year	3851
Average of last 3 years	3961
Average lifetime	3312
Average of best 10 years	4762
Average of best 15 years	4592
Average of best 20 years	4419

Note: The earnings are all in terms of 1973 prices.

the average of a number of selected best years, but that of the best twenty years is seen to be just over £1000 larger than that of annual average lifetime earnings; that is 33 per cent more! It is also almost £500 more than that of the final three years.

The sensitivity of these results to the assumed process of year to year relative earnings changes used in the simulations is examined in appendix B, where it is shown that the results are robust.

The immediate implication of this result is of course that the anticipated increases in contributions rates required to finance a mature British pension scheme are too optimistic. It is therefore anticipated that contributions will be increased by more than originally planned, or that the value of pensions will be reduced. A simple method of effectively reducing pensions is to fail to increase the basic minimum pension by the full extent of inflation. It will be interesting to see how long pensions remain inflation proof in future.

However, comparisons of pensionable earnings provide only one element in the estimation of total pension costs. The simulation model must also be extended to cover the benefits received over retirement, and this is considered in the following section.

FURTHER SIMULATION RESULTS

The previous section has shown that the values of earnings on which the earnings-related pensions are based are substantially higher when a number of selected best years are used instead of a lifetime average. Nevertheless, the implications of this result for the total costs of the benefits which have to be paid are far from clear. These costs will of course depend on the nature of the actual benefit formula, the distribution of the average of the best twenty years in the population, and the distribution of the duration of the period of retirement. The distribution of the average of the best twenty years earnings will influence the number of individuals who are affected by the upper limit to the pension.

Furthermore, if those with relatively high pensionable earnings tend, on average, to live longer than those with relatively low earnings, the costs will be higher than if death rates are unrelated to earnings.

The pension formula

Consider first the effect of the pension formula, and as before the following analysis relates to the single person only. Now in the original White Paper of 1974 the values of the basic pension and the upper limit were set at £10 and £70 per week respectively. In the later 'Explanatory Memorandum' of 1975 these values were altered to £11·60 and £80, while at the introduction of the scheme in April 1978 they were £17·50 and £120 per week. These adjustments have clearly been made in line with the general increase in prices over the period, and future increases, at least in line with the cost of living, are explicit in the new pension legislation. It would therefore seem that for present purposes it would be sufficient to adjust to 1973 prices (since the simulated earnings for the cohort born in 1943 are in constant 1973 prices). But this would give annual values of £442 and £3120 respectively for the basic pension and the upper earnings limit, and it is immediately obvious that these figures are much too low. From table 4.1 it can be seen that the upper limit would be below annual average lifetime earnings.

The reason why this straightforward adjustment is not appropriate is that in obtaining these values no allowance has been made for the important phenomenon of overtaking whereby younger cohorts earn more at comparable ages than older cohorts.[1] The values in 1978 may have been appropriate for the cohort which had just retired, but when later cohorts (who have higher earnings at every stage in their life cycle, and pay higher contributions) retire, it will clearly be necessary to raise the limits by more than the increase in prices. When the cohort used for the present simulations retires at age 65, it will be the year 2008. A more realistic adjustment would therefore ensure that the upper earnings limit bears an appropriate relationship to the earnings of the cohort which is due to retire.[2] In fact a comparison of the above values of the upper limit with the average earnings of men in the age group 60–65 years shows that the ratio of the former to the latter is approximately 1·45. Applying this ratio to the simulated earnings of the cohort born in 1943 gives an appropriate upper limit of £5600 (in 1973 prices) for the year in which they retire. This implies a basic minimum pension of £800 per year,

---

[1] This is discussed in more detail in Creedy and Hart, 'Age and the distribution of earnings'.
[2] The fact that the simulations are based on such earnings limits means that the model does not represent the full complexity of the new state scheme. But the above argument strongly suggests that an adjustment using only prices would not be reasonable in a mature scheme, even without productivity and other 'time' effects, because of the typical shape of the age-earnings profile.

which is calculated as one seventh of the upper limit (the fact that the upper limit is approximately seven times as large as the basic pension has been discussed in chapter 3). When these values are combined with an earnings-related proportional rate of 0·25, the highest annual pension is seen to be £2000 (obtained from 800 + 0·25 (5600 − 800)).[1]

Some idea of the effect of this pension formula on costs may be illustrated by comparing the annual pension of the hypothetical individual who has the arithmetic mean value of annual average lifetime earnings (of £3312 from table 4.1), with the pension based on the arithmetic mean of the average of the best twenty years' earnings (of £4419). In the former case the pension would be £1428, while in the latter case it would be £1706; that is, 19·4 per cent higher. While the value of earnings on which the pension is based is 33 per cent higher, the difference between the annual pensions is therefore much lower. But of course the average annual pension is not equal to the pension based on average earnings, since the distribution of pensionable earnings is of crucial importance.

Differential mortality

It has been suggested that the total pension costs depend to some extent on rates of mortality, and in particular on the extent to which individuals with high lifetime earnings may on average live longer than those with relatively low lifetime earnings. There are unfortunately very few data which can be used to examine this question directly. Some information about differential mortality is available, but it is classified by occupation (that is, the occupation which is recorded on the death certificate). What is required here is information about mortality rates classified by lifetime earnings. However the survival curve which shows the proportion of individuals who survive to any given age from, say, 65 years, may easily be obtained from demographic statistics.

The approach taken here, then, is to obtain a simulated age of death for each individual in such a way that the resulting survival curve is approximately the same as that for males in Great Britain. Although there is necessarily a large random element in the determination of the age at death, there is imposed on the simulations a slight tendency for those with lifetime earnings which are above the average to live longer than average. The expectation of life at age 65 is approximately twelve years, and in carrying out the simulations no individual is assumed to live beyond the age of 90 years. Further details of the model of differential mortality are given in appendix B.

---

[1] The pension formula clearly involves different replacement rates at different income levels, but this does not allow direct inferences to be made about the redistribution of lifetime income. This question is discussed in chapter 5.

Discounted value of pensions

The next stage of the analysis is to calculate for each individual the discounted value of his pension from retirement until death, using the pension formula corresponding to the new pension scheme. This can be done for each of the earnings bases shown in table 4.1 above. Arithmetic means of the distribution of discounted pensions for each earnings base, using a real rate of interest of 5 per cent, are given in table 4.2. This is a rather high real rate, but the main purpose of the calculations is to compare the costs of schemes which use different earnings bases, and these comparisons were not affected by the rate of interest. The dispersion of the distributions is considered at a later stage, in chapter 5.

From table 4.2 it can be seen that when each individual's pension is based on his average earnings over the best twenty years, the arithmetic mean discounted pension is 13 per cent higher than if each individual's pension were based on his annual average lifetime earnings. The corresponding difference for a pension based on the best ten years is 16 per cent. It is important to note that these comparisons are not sensitive to rates of interest, which is why the results for only one rate have been presented here.

A major reason why the difference in total pension costs between lifetime and selective averaging is lower than the difference between the earnings bases is that a significant proportion of individuals is affected by the upper limit to the pension. It is therefore worth comparing the two-tier scheme with a simple earnings-related pension scheme; that is, one with no basic minimum or upper earnings limit. In this case it is found that the average discounted pension for earnings-related schemes based on earnings in the final year, the average of the best ten years, and of the best twenty years, exceeds that based on annual average earnings by 17 per cent, 44 per cent and 34 per cent respectively. These are much larger than for the two-tier scheme because of the absence of the upper limit, and are slightly larger than the differences between the earnings

Table 4.2. *Arithmetic means of alternative distributions of discounted pensions*

Earnings base	Arithmetic mean £s
Final year	13002
Average last 3 years	13159
Average lifetime	12490
Average best 10 years	14526
Average best 15 years	14334
Average best 20 years	14123

Notes: (i) Values are in 1973 prices
       (ii) Real rate of interest = 5 per cent

bases of table 4.1 because of the tendency for the higher earners to live, on average, slightly longer than the lower earners.

Accumulated value of contributions

It is also possible to use the simulations to examine separately the effect of the upper earnings limit on total contributions. The calculations for the state scheme use an upper limit on earnings of £5600, and combined employee plus employer contributions of 16·5 per cent. Maximum annual contributions are therefore £924. Using these values with the simulated age-earnings profiles it was possible to calculate the total accumulated value of contributions, from age 20 to retirement at age 65 years. This value was then compared with the total accumulated value of contributions under a scheme with simple proportional contributions of the same rate but without the upper earnings limit. It was found that the former was 4·4 per cent lower than the latter using a rate of interest of 5 per cent per year. The upper limit therefore has a substantial effect on contributions, and this aspect of the limit is examined further in chapter 7.

CONCLUSIONS

This chapter has examined some of the effects of basing earnings-related pensions on the average earnings of the best twenty years of working life, rather than on average lifetime earnings or other measures of pensionable earnings. The analysis was based on the simulated earnings over the working life of a single cohort of individuals born in 1943, where the simulations were obtained using a realistic model of age-earnings profiles which explicitly deals with the extent to which individuals' earnings typically fluctuate from year to year. It was shown that the arithmetic mean value of the distribution of the average of the best twenty years' earnings was approximately one third greater than that of average life earnings when measured at constant prices with general real earnings growth of about 2 per cent per annum. This is greater than the assumption made by the Government Actuary, but it is of course extremely difficult to assess the extent to which this affects the other calculations reported in the various White Papers.

When allowance is made for the pension formula and differential mortality of those who reach pension age, total benefits discounted to age 65 were found to be approximately 13 per cent greater under the new two-tier scheme than under a scheme where pensionable earnings are calculated as average lifetime earnings. These results suggest that it will be difficult for governments to maintain contribution rates and pensions at the planned levels.

In the preparation of the calculations it also became clear that the decision to adjust the pension levels (the flat-rate pension and upper limit) using a price index, rather than an index of average earnings, would result over a long period in levels which are too low relative to the contributions paid during working life by those reaching retirement age. This is not simply a consequence of productivity growth but arises because of the fact, displayed by the longitudinal data used to estimate the model of age-earnings profiles, that the younger cohorts earn more at comparable ages than the older cohorts.

The ultimate choice of the type of pension system and the choice of values for policy variables will, of course, depend not only on the desired minimum level of pensions or prescribed levels of income replacement in old age for the higher earners, but will also be influenced by explicit judgement about the desired amount of redistribution. Discussions of pensions have often paid little attention to the question of redistribution, and have often concentrated on the nature of the pension formula alone. The implications of alternative pension schemes for the redistribution of lifetime income are therefore considered in the next chapter.

PENSIONS AND REDISTRIBUTION

It has been shown in chapter 3 that the types of policy choices which are available under flat-rate and earnings-related schemes are very different, in particular that the relationships between contributions and benefits are significantly altered. The choice in favour of earnings-related pensions implies very different fundamental objectives from those implied by the choice of flat-rate pensions, although it was suggested that previous policy decisions have not always shown consistency.

The desire to achieve a particular basic minimum pension, or to provide certain replacement rates for higher earners within a state scheme, is of course associated with attitudes towards the redistribution of income. Some people may regard redistribution as an objective in itself, and will choose the scheme which implies the greatest amount of redistribution from rich to poor, subject to the usual constraints relating to the finance of the scheme. Others may however regard redistribution itself as an important constraint on the choice of pension system, rather than as an objective. In either case it is obviously necessary to have a quantitative measure of the likely amount of redistribution implied by any scheme, though unfortunately very few studies have been made which relate to Great Britain. The author of one of these studies states clearly that: 'Unless the redistributional aspects are clearly and fully set out, it is totally impossible to discuss with any semblance of rationality whether such changes should be additional to, or in substitution for, the various other redistributional activities of the public sector.'[1]

The purpose of this chapter is therefore to examine the redistributive implications of various types of pension scheme. The interpretation of redistribution in the context of pension schemes is not however immediately clear, and is discussed first. The second section then makes

---

[1] A. R. Prest, 'Some redistributional aspects of the National Superannuation fund', *Three Banks Review*, no. 86, June 1970, p. 17. The same scheme is examined in A. B. Atkinson, 'National superannuation: redistribution and value for money', *Oxford Bulletin of Economics and Statistics*, vol. 32, 1970. See also Titmuss, *Social Policy*. More work has been carried out in the United States, a useful study being that of H. Aaron, 'Demographic effects on the equity of Social Security benefits', in M. S. Feldstein and R. P. Inman (eds.), *The Economics of Public Services*, London, Macmillan, 1977. An earlier contribution is J. A. Brittain, *The Payroll Tax for Social Security*, Washington DC, Brookings Institution, 1973, especially chapter VI.

some general comparisons using the framework of analysis described in chapter 3. It was shown in the second section of chapter 3 that different schemes involve different relationships between individuals' earnings and rates of return from the state pension, but the second section of this chapter provides direct measures of the redistribution involved in each scheme. The third section then uses the simulation model of chapter 4 to examine the implications for redistribution of earnings variability and differential mortality. These results enable a number of qualifications to be made to the results of the second section.

INTER-GENERATIONAL AND INTRA-GENERATIONAL REDISTRIBUTION

Any state pension scheme which provides a pension which is related only partially to an average of earnings over a period of time (irrespective of the time profile of contributions), and which is paid during an indefinite length of time, will inevitably involve a considerable amount of *ex post* redistribution of income. In other words virtually every individual would find, at the end of his life, that the accumulated value of his contributions was not equal to the lump sum which would have been necessary to finance his pension during retirement. Some, mainly those who live longest and pay the bulk of their contributions late in working life, would gain at the expense of others. But this statement then raises two further questions. First, there is the question of the extent to which those in one generation of pensioners may actually gain *in aggregate* at the expense of the current generation of workers, even after allowing for their own possible subsidy towards the previous generation of pensioners. Secondly, there is the question of the extent to which the imbalance mentioned above is more or less evenly spread over the people within each generation, or whether there is more systematic redistribution. Even if every member of one generation were indebted to the subsequent generation, the question of the distribution of the net gains obviously remains.

The first of these two issues relates to *inter*-generational redistribution, while the second is concerned with *intra*-generational redistribution. Now some inter-generational redistribution is inevitable with a pay-as-you-go system, especially where benefits are adjusted according to past rates of inflation and growth of real earnings. The amount of such aggregate redistribution between groups will depend among other things on the extent to which inflation, population growth and productivity change at an uneven rate over time. This is because three generations are involved in the calculation of the net subsidy to the middle generation. These factors are largely outside the scope of the present study. But it should be mentioned that the concept of a 'generation' is not precise. Since there are large variations in both the working and the retired lives of people who are born in the same year, there is in practice considerable over-lapping between generations.

This chapter therefore concentrates on *intra*-generational redistribution. As in chapters 3 and 4, it should again be clear that this question can only be examined in the context of the lifetime incomes of a particular cohort of individuals. It is also important to identify this type of redistribution, since judgement about its desirability will depend on considerations which are quite different from those concerning *inter*-generational redistribution.

SOME GENERAL COMPARISONS

There is a vast number of factors which affect the possible extent of systematic redistribution involved in different pension schemes. Because of the complexity of this problem, it seems useful to begin here by considering the implications of the various types of contribution and benefit schemes in isolation from some of the complicating factors such as earnings variability over life and differential mortality. This section therefore uses the framework of analysis described in chapter 3. The third section of this chapter then uses the simulation model described in chapter 4.

Dispersion of gross and net lifetime income

A convenient method of obtaining a preliminary impression of redistribution is to compare a measure of the dispersion of discounted net income (that is, income after the subtraction of contributions and payment of pensions) with that of the dispersion of gross lifetime income. This is in fact the method adopted in this section and, in the context of the two period framework outlined in chapter 3 and used here (where life consists of a working period followed by a retirement period), it is only necessary to discount the single pension payment back to the working period. For each individual, net income during the first period is simply the difference between earnings and contributions to the pension fund. The only source of income during the retirement period is of course the pension financed from the fund. The pension is discounted back to the first period using the same interest factor as that applied to the pension fund.[1] It is worth pointing out that no attempt has been made to

---

[1] Calculations were also made using undiscounted lifetime income, but the comparisons between alternative schemes are not affected.

consider a distribution of welfare, or to allow for such factors as differences in rates of time preference between individuals. The purpose of this chapter is simply to obtain a descriptive measure of the dispersion of net income, and to compare this with the dispersion of earnings obtained in the working period.

Using the model of chapter 3 then, it is clear that a scheme which uses directly proportional contributions and benefits will not involve any redistribution. The rate of return from the scheme is the same for all individuals, and is equal to the rate of interest obtained by the pension fund. This conclusion will, of course, need to be modified when earnings fluctuations and differential mortality are considered in the following section. However, where the pension is proportional to income averaged over the whole period, it is easy to see that redistribution will only be caused by differential rates of mortality between individuals in different income groups.

Proportional contributions with flat-rate pension

If, however, proportional contributions are levied on earnings while a flat-rate pension is paid, there must be a certain amount of redistribution from the relatively high to the relatively low earners. This can be seen from chart 3.4 which shows that those with earnings above the arithmetic mean obtain a rate of return from the scheme which is lower than the rate of interest obtained by the fund, and vice versa for those below the arithmetic mean.

The reduction in inequality brought about by this type of scheme may also be seen as follows. The use of a constant proportional contributions rate (with no earnings limits) means that the relative dispersion of post-contribution earnings during working life is the same as that of gross earnings; each individual's earnings are simply reduced by the same percentage amount. But the payment of a flat-rate pension increases each individual's net lifetime income by the same *absolute* amount, and this must obviously represent a higher *proportion* of earnings for the lower than for the higher earners. The relative dispersion of net income is therefore lower than that of earnings. The extent of redistribution increases as the rate of proportional contributions increases since it is then possible to pay a higher flat-rate pension (as shown in chapter 3).

Proportional contributions with two-tier pension

The case of proportional contributions with a two-tier pension is rather more complex, though the method of analysis proceeds as before by considering the relationship between discounted net income and earnings in the working period, for individuals in different ranges of the distribution of gross earnings. Where there are no earnings limits for

contributions or for pensions, the population must effectively be divided
into two components. The treatment of those with earnings below the
level of the flat-rate pension is similar to that discussed in the previous
section; the net effect of the scheme is to reduce relative dispersion
within this group.

For those with earnings above the lower limit the relationship between
gross earnings during working life and the pension received in the
retirement period can easily be obtained; the same formula applies to
everyone in this group. There is therefore some income redistribution
within each of these two groups, but it is also important to realise that
there is redistribution *between* the groups, since all of those with earnings
below the basic pension have a higher income during retirement than
during working life.

The dispersion of the discounted net income over the population as a
whole must therefore be obtained by a suitable combination of the three
components; the two within-group components and a component arising
from redistribution between the groups. For this reason it is necessary to
use a measure of relative dispersion which is capable of being decom-
posed into a number of separate components. It is also necessary to use a
measure such that if there is a simple transformation between earnings
and discounted net income (within any group in the population), it must
also be possible to derive a tractable relationship between the relative
dispersions of the two distributions. With these considerations in mind,
the most convenient measure of dispersion to use is the coefficient of
variation (obtained as the ratio of the standard deviation to the
arithmetic mean).

In the case of the two-tier pension with upper earnings limits to both
the contributions and pensionable earnings, then of course the population must be divided into three groups; the additional group contains
those individuals with earnings above the upper limit. There is some
redistribution within the three groups, but there are now three between
group components to be considered (for example, with groups 1, 2 and
3, there is redistribution between groups 1 and 2, between 1 and 3, and
between 2 and 3). The method of analysis is therefore slightly more
cumbersome, but proceeds as before. Further details concerning the
calculation of the measure of dispersion are given in appendix A.

Diagrammatic comparisons

Comparisons between alternative two-tier pension schemes, with proportional contributions, can be made most conveniently using diagrams.
Thus chart 5.1 shows the relationship between the coefficient of
variation of discounted net income and the proportional pension rate
used in the upper tier. Examples are given for two different values of the

basic pension, for a system without upper earnings limits, and for two
different values of the ratio of the upper earnings limit to the basic
pension. For example the line marked AB in chart 5.1 represents a
two-tier scheme with a basic pension of 15 per cent of average earnings
and an upper earnings limit of seven times the basic pension (which is
the ratio used in the British scheme). The bottom line of chart 5.1,
marked CD, illustrates the case of a two-tier scheme with no upper
earnings limit and a higher basic pension of 22 per cent of average
earnings. It is worth noting that the relationship between the coefficient
of variation of discounted net income and the proportional pension rate
is linear, although it is by no means obvious that this should turn out to
be the case. The intercept on the vertical axis, where the proportional
pension rate is zero, gives the relative dispersion for a system with only a
flat-rate pension. The earnings limit, where appropriate, must therefore
be regarded as applying only to earnings-related contributions. In
examining chart 5.1 it should be remembered that the coefficient of
variation of the distribution of earnings used in the calculations is 0.471
(the assumptions about the distribution are discussed in more detail in
chapter 3).

In interpreting the results presented in chart 5.1 it is most important
to stress that variations in the policy parameters (the proportional
pension rate and basic minimum pension) are being considered in the
context of a self-financing scheme in which any increase in the proportional pension rate must be matched by an appropriate increase in the
contributions rate, for which reference may be made to charts 3.2 and
3.3 of chapter 3. Increases in the proportional pension rate would
otherwise result in larger increases in the coefficient of variation of
discounted net income. The results of chapter 3 showed that as the
proportional pension rate in the upper tier increases, substantial increases in the contributions rate are required in order to ensure that the
scheme is self-financing. Since the burden of the higher contributions
falls proportionately more heavily on those with earnings below the
upper limit, the dispersion of discounted net income is less unequal than
it would be if contributions remained unchanged. Although, for example, the line AB slopes upwards as replacement rates are increased for
the higher earners, the gradient is rather small.

The values in chart 5.1 may be compared with the coefficient of
variation of discounted net income resulting from a system which
combines earnings-related contributions (with no upper limit) with a
flat-rate pension only. Using the same rate of interest it is found that
coefficient of variation is equal to 0.404 and 0.375 respectively, for a
flat-rate pension of 15 and 22 per cent of average earnings. These values
are substantially below points E and C respectively in chart 5.1,

Chart 5.1. *Dispersion of discounted net income*

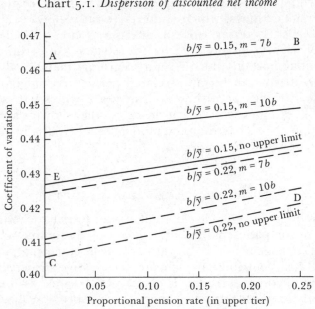

Note: Interest factor = 1·6.
KEY
b = basic minimum pension
$\bar{y}$ = arithmetic mean earnings (£5431)
m = upper earnings limit

demonstrating the extent to which an upper earnings limit on contributions (even without earnings-related pensions) reduces the redistributive potential of pensions.

The results of the analysis, summarised in chart 5.1, show that the dispersion of discounted net income is very sensitive to two ratios. First, relative dispersion is reduced substantially as the ratio of the basic pension to arithmetic mean earnings is increased (compare the continuous lines of chart 5.1 with the lower dashed lines for higher basic pensions). Secondly, relative dispersion is reduced as the ratio of the upper earnings limit to the basic pension is increased. It is important to stress that these comparisons are not sensitive to the rate of interest used in the calculations.

Now the British legislation, as outlined in chapter 2, is framed in terms of the upper earnings limit being approximately seven times the basic pension, and approximately one and a half times the value of average earnings. This implies that the basic pension is only about one fifth of average earnings, which is therefore rather low.[1]

It is, however, necessary to examine the extent to which the above results may need to be modified by the existence of earnings mobility and differential mortality. Furthermore, earnings mobility allows for the possibility of basing an earnings-related pension on different values of pensionable earnings according to the years which are selected for averaging. These questions are considered in the following section, using the simulation results based on the model described briefly in chapter 4, and in more detail in appendix B.

FURTHER SIMULATION RESULTS

Before examining the possible extent of overall systematic redistribution, it is useful to compare separately the effects of alternative contributions and benefit arrangements. It has already been noted that with a strict earnings-related contributions scheme the relative dispersion of post-contribution lifetime earnings is exactly the same as that of pre-contribution earnings. But when there is an upper limit beyond which the marginal contributions rate is zero, then the dispersion of post-contribution earnings will necessarily exceed that of gross earnings. In fact, for the new government scheme (using the value of the upper earnings limit of £5600 for the simulated cohort 1943) the coefficient of variation of the distribution of annual average post-contribution earnings over life is 0·466, which may be compared with a value of 0·441 for the distribution of annual average gross earnings.

Dispersion of accumulated contributions

However, this comparison takes no account of the time stream of earnings, and the extent to which this differs between individuals. Two people may obtain the same annual average earnings over life and also live to the same age, but the person who pays a larger proportion of his contributions early in working life would be entitled, on actuarial considerations, to a larger pension. Now in fact there is a tendency for those with relatively higher lifetime earnings to reach their peak earnings at a relatively older age than those with lower lifetime earnings, and this phenomenon is also reflected in the simulation model used in

---

[1] It should be remembered that the analysis carried out in this section does not use a lower earnings limit (equal to the basic pension) below which individuals need not pay contributions. In fact the payment of contributions on such low earnings is voluntary in the new state scheme introduced in 1978, but individuals must pay contributions in order to retain eligibility for full pension benefits.

this study.[1] It is therefore of interest to consider the dispersion of accumulated contributions from age 20 to age 65.

The simulations show that for a scheme using directly proportional contributions, the coefficient of variation of accumulated contributions up to retirement is equal to 0·379 for a rate of interest of 5 per cent. (The dispersion is lower when the rate of interest is higher, but the particular comparisons made here are not affected by the rate of interest). For the two-tier scheme, with an upper earnings limit on contributions, the corresponding value is lower at 0·303. Not surprisingly the effect of the upper limit is therefore to lower the dispersion of accumulated contributions.

Dispersion of discounted benefits

Turning to the consideration of benefits in alternative schemes, it has already been noted that the dispersion of pensions discounted back to the date of retirement would not be expected to equal the dispersion of accumulated contributions. The former will depend on the dispersion of the earnings measure on which the pension is based (pensionable earnings), the values of the basic pension and upper earnings limit, and on the nature of differential mortality. Alternative values of the dispersion of the distribution of discounted pensions for the simulated cohort 1943 are given in table 5.1. Results are presented for a directly proportional pension and for the two-tier scheme.[2]

Comparisons may then be made with the dispersion of accumulated contributions given in the previous section. It can be seen that in every

Table 5.1. *Dispersion of pensions discounted to retirement*

	Coefficient of variation	
	Proportional pension	Two-tier scheme
Pensionable earnings in:		
Final year	0·808	0·496
Average last 3 years	0·803	0·492
Average lifetime	0·651	0·478
Average best 10 years	0·721	0·465
Average best 15 years	0·715	0·467
Average best 20 years	0·707	0·469

Note: Rate of interest = 5 per cent

[1] The model of life earnings used here was fitted to data covering all occupations combined, so that although the statement in the text is true the phenomenon may not be fully covered by the simulations.

[2] The proportional contributions rate used for the analysis of the state scheme was 16·5 per cent of earnings, as in chapter 4. For the proportional scheme (no earnings limits) the precise value of the contributions rate is not relevant.

case the dispersion of the distribution of discounted pensions is considerably greater than that of accumulated contributions. However, the dispersion with the new government scheme is substantially lower than with a proportional scheme, because of the effect of both the basic minimum pension and the upper earnings limit. It can also be seen that with the two-tier scheme the dispersion of discounted pensions using the average of the best ten years' earnings is no longer greater than that using the average of the twenty best years. This is obviously because more people are affected by the upper pension limit.

Pension–contribution ratios

These results show that there is a wide dispersion across individuals in the ratio of discounted benefits to accumulated contributions. One method of examining the overall redistributive impact of the pension scheme is to relate the pension–contributions ratio to annual average lifetime earnings. A scheme involving systematic redistribution from relatively high to relatively low lifetime earners would be expected to show a significant negative relationship, such that higher values of annual average life earnings are associated with relatively lower values of the ratio of the discounted pension to accumulated contributions.

The relationship may be examined more formally using regression analysis. Regressions of the pension-contribution ratio on the logarithm of annual average lifetime earnings are reported in table 5.2 for both a proportional pension scheme and for the two-tier scheme. All examples are for an interest rate of 5 per cent.

Table 5.2 *Regressions of pension–contribution ratio on logarithm of average lifetime earnings*

	Proportional scheme		Two-tier scheme	
	Regression coefficient	r^2	Regression coefficient	r^2
Pensionable earnings in:				
Final year	0·447 (0·052)	0·446	−0·004 (0·012)	0·017
Average last 3 years	0·463 (0·052)	0·459	−0·004 (0·012)	0·019
Average lifetime	0·028 (0·038)	0·303	−0·013 (0.011)	0·009
Average best 10 years	0·427 (0·056)	0·401	−0·024 (0·013)	0·105
Average best 15 years	0·406 (0·054)	0·397	−0·021 (0·013)	0·095
Average best 20 years	0·379 (0·052)	0·391	−0·019 (0·013)	0·086

It can be seen from table 5.2 that for the scheme which uses proportional contributions *and* benefits (with no earnings limits), the regression coefficients are all significantly positive. There is a fairly wide dispersion around the regression line, as indicated by the values of r^2. These results therefore indicate that such a scheme would be regressive, irrespective of the method used to calculate pensionable earnings. Where pensionable earnings are simply average lifetime earnings, it has already been noted that the scheme would be regressive to the extent that longevity is positively related to lifetime earnings and that there is a tendency for the higher earners to obtain peak earnings relatively later in their working life. Table 5.2 shows that the other methods of calculating pensionable earnings involve substantially more redistribution from poor to rich.

The results shown in table 5.2 for the two-tier scheme indicate that pension–contributions ratios are negatively related to the logarithm of average lifetime earnings, implying a small amount of redistribution from rich to poor. However the extent of systematic redistribution involved is very small.[1]

It is also of interest to examine corresponding results for the two-tier scheme, but using a higher ratio of the upper earnings limit to the basic minimum pension. Results using the higher ratio of ten are therefore given in table 5.3, again using a rate of interest of 5 per cent.

Table 5.3. *Regressions of pension–contributions ratio on logarithms of average lifetime earnings*

	Regression coefficient	r^2
Pensionable earnings in:		
Final year	−0·025	0·120
	(0·012)	
Average last 3 years	−0·025	0·121
	(0·012)	
Average lifetime	−0·034	0·180
	(0·012)	
Average best 10 years	−0·045	0·197
	(0·013)	
Average best 15 years	−0·043	0·188
	(0·013)	
Average best 20 years	−0·040	0·182
	(0·013)	

Note: Two-tier scheme but with $m = 10b$

[1] In the study mentioned on page 36n comparisons were made between measures of dispersion of discounted lifetime earnings and discounted net income (after the payment of contributions and the receipt of pension). In all cases the latter were only marginally lower than the former, supporting the results obtained above.

Comparison with table 5.2 shows that raising the upper limit on both contributions and benefits increases the extent of systematic redistribution (as would be expected from the results of the second section of this chapter) which nevertheless remains very low.

CONCLUSIONS

This chapter has considered the possible extent of intra-generational redistribution implied by a number of alternative state pension schemes. As in chapters 3 and 4, the analysis was confined to a single cohort of individuals, of which all members reach pension age. Simple comparisons, which abstract from earnings variability over life and from differential mortality, showed that schemes similar to the new government scheme involve substantially less systematic redistribution than the alternatives considered. When simulations are used to allow for the fact that earnings fluctuate from year to year and that there is a tendency for higher earners to live on average relatively longer than lower earners, a scheme like the current state scheme was seen to result in very little systematic redistribution. The emphasis here must be on the word systematic, since there is a considerable amount of variation in the implied rate of return received by individuals.

It should be repeated that the analysis has ignored the possible effects of benefits for dependents, and of death-in-service benefits to widows. Furthermore, it has not been possible to consider here the extent of eligibility for full pension benefits, although repeated sickness and unemployment over working life will ultimately affect an individual's pension rights on retirement. The fact that in recent years an increasing proportion of pensioners has been reliant on supplementary benefits has been well documented.[1]

An important feature of the 1975 pension legislation which has not so far been considered is the facility for certain groups of individuals to contract out of the state scheme. The extent to which contracting out may affect both the relationship between contributions and benefits, and the redistributive nature of alternative schemes, is examined in the next chapter.

---

[1] For further discussion and references see J. Creedy and R. Disney, 'Eligibility for unemployment benefits in Great Britain', *Oxford Economic Papers*, vol. 33, no. 2, 1981.

6

PUBLIC AND PRIVATE PENSION SCHEMES

A major feature of the new British pension scheme which has not so far been examined is the ability to contract out of the earnings-related pension. As outlined in chapter 2, individuals continue to retain membership of the state scheme insofar as they pay (reduced) contributions and receive the basic minimum pension on retirement. The scheme is therefore referred to as one of partial contracting out. Contracting out in this form represents, along with the rule for averaging earnings over the best twenty years to calculate pensionable earnings, a significant departure from previous practice. Indeed, the Second Permanent Secretary in the Department of Health and Social Security wrote, 'We are attempting something which, to my knowledge, is paralleled nowhere in the western world'.[1] Because of the radical nature of the scheme, the difficulties of predicting the number of employees who are likely to be contracted out are therefore formidable, and experience with the scheme has been too short to serve as a useful guide. However, the facility for some individuals to be contracted out of the scheme has important implications for the benefits which can be financed by those retaining full membership. The purpose of this chapter is therefore to examine some of these implications, in particular the extent to which contracting out introduces additional and serious constraints on the policy choices available.

First, it is necessary to discuss some details of the new state scheme relating to contracting out, and some general principles which must apply to any scheme which allows either full or partial contracting out. This is followed by an examination of the implications, for the relationship between benefits and contributions, of contracting out. This section provides a comparison between a scheme which is in many respects similar to the state system, and one which combines earnings-related contributions with a flat-rate pension and *full* contracting out. As in previous chapters it is necessary to abstract from many complicating elements, and this chapter again uses the framework of analysis which was presented in chapter 3. The third section then examines the extent to which the redistributive ability of various schemes is affected by

[1] See J. A. Atkinson, 'The developing relationship between the state pension scheme and occupational pension schemes', *Social and Economic Administration, 11*, no. 3, 1977, p. 225.

contracting out. In particular, it is necessary to examine the claim made by the Second Permanent Secretary to the Department of Health and Social Security, that 'it proved possible to devise contracting out systems which left the redistributive and subsidy element of the state scheme more or less intact'.[1]

The new arrangements have often been referred to as a partnership with private pension schemes. Indeed, they have provided a considerable boost to the private pension industry. Because private schemes are to a large extent funded (although the requirement that contracted out schemes be indexed creates large management problems) their growth has meant that the investments of insurance companies have grown significantly in recent years. The implications of this growth present an important subject of study, but they cannot be examined here.

CONTRACTING OUT OF THE 1978 PENSION SCHEME

The introduction of an option to contract out of the second tier of the new government scheme raises extremely complex problems and, as with the other issues, only a small number of relevant aspects can be considered here. The decision on whether or not to contract out actually rests with the employer, who must apply to the Occupational Pensions Board, which will ensure that the alternative scheme provided by the employer satisfies certain requirements. A major criterion is that employees must be at least as well-off with the private scheme as they would be with the state scheme. Thus, a requirement is that pensions in the private schemes must also be adjusted for inflation. Although the government has accepted some responsibility for such adjustments it is clear that formidable financial problems are raised.

The obligation to support private schemes using general exchequer revenue also raises a question relating to the distribution of the tax burden. This is because the superannuation contributions to a private scheme of those who are contracted out are subtracted from their gross earnings along with their other allowances before their taxable incomes are obtained. However, the whole of the National Insurance contributions of individuals who are not contracted out are included in taxable income. This issue is considered in more detail in chapter 7 and in appendix C, but it is difficult to see the justification for this asymmetric treatment of what are regarded by the state as compulsory savings for retirement.

The fact that employers are responsible for alternative schemes introduces a further range of problems associated with labour mobility

[1] Ibid, p. 216.

and the transfer of pension rights, and although this is covered by the new pension legislation, there have been a number of serious criticisms of the possible disincentive effects of the arrangements. Furthermore, since the initiative rests with the employer the problem of predicting the number of individuals who are likely to be involved in contracted out schemes becomes very difficult. The decision may well depend on the nature of the firm or organisation, and may not always be closely related to the level or stability of earnings and employment of the employees (although not all of an employer's labour force need be contracted out).

Incentives to contract out and differential contributions

These administratives features of the contracting out arrangements are of course important, but the primary task here is to examine the nature of the individual incentives to contract out. Now an obvious but fundamental point to stress about contracting out is that in any state scheme where the relatively higher earners anticipate a rate of return from the scheme which is lower than that of the lower earners, and lower than the market rate of interest, there is an incentive to contract out. But if those individuals are completely free to contract out without continuing to contribute to the state scheme, then more and more people would contract out as the benefits which can be financed in the scheme are progressively reduced. Thus a state pension scheme which allows any kind of contracting out must impose what may be called differential contributions on those contracting out, simply in order to ensure the survival of the state scheme for any individuals other than the very lowest earners.

The nature of the differential contributions imposed by the British scheme may conveniently be illustrated using the schedule of benefits and contributions, expressed in current annual values, which operated when the scheme was first introduced in April 1978. Details are shown in table 6.1 for those in the mature scheme; that is, such individuals are assumed to have contributed for at least twenty years. It should of course be stressed that the special contributions arrangements for those contracted out do not imply that those individuals are in any sense worse off.

In 1978 total contributions for individuals contracted into the new scheme were made up of employee and employer contributions of $6\frac{1}{2}$ per cent and 10 per cent of earnings respectively up to the limit of £6240 per year. The contributions schedule for those contracted out is slightly more complex, being the same as for those contracted in, on earnings up to the basic minimum pension of £910, and 4 per cent and $5\frac{1}{2}$ per cent of earnings between £910 and £6240 for employee and employer

Table 6.1. *Contributions and benefits: new pension scheme* (£s)

Annual average earnings	Single pension	Total contributions Contracted-in	Contracted-out
910	910	150	150
1820	1139	300	237
2600	1334	429	310
4000	1724	686	459
5460	2049	901	582
6240+	2244	1030	657

Note: All values are for the scheme at April 1978, in current prices, and are rounded to the nearest £1.

respectively.[1] It should be noted that although the question of the incidence of the employer's contribution to pensions is very important in other contexts, it is not necessary for the purposes of the present illustrations to consider this problem.

A crucial feature of the contracting out arrangements is immediately clear from the schedule of contributions of those who opt out of the earnings-related upper tier of the new pension scheme. Although they are only entitled to the basic minimum pension of £910 per year, they must nevertheless pay contributions in addition to those which would be required by an individual with earnings such that he is only just eligible for the basic minimum. The total contributions of $9\frac{1}{2}$ per cent of earnings between £910 and £6240 may therefore be regarded as differential contributions which are levied on the earnings of those contracting out. Such differential contributions are a vital element of any pension scheme in which there is an incentive, and facility, for individuals to contract out; indeed, they are necessary if schemes are to remain viable.

Consider an individual with regular earnings of £4000 per year. From table 6.1 it can be seen that he and his employer would contribute £686 per year into the state scheme, in return for an annual pension on retirement of £1724. Now an individual with regular earnings equal to the basic pension of £910 would pay, in combination with his employer, annual contributions of £150 (calculated as $16\frac{1}{2}$ per cent of £910). If the hypothetical individual with earnings of £4000 wishes partially to contract out of the state scheme and receive only a basic state pension on retirement, he must nevertheless pay more than £150 as contributions to the state scheme. In fact table 6.1 shows that contributions of £459 would have to be paid. It would therefore only be possible for the

[1] These rates do not include the National Insurance surcharge imposed on employers' contributions. Employees' contracted in and contracted out rates in June 1980 were $6\frac{3}{4}$ per cent and $4\frac{1}{4}$ per cent respectively.

individual to transfer £227 per year (calculated as £686–£459) to an alternative fund, rather than £536, which is the difference between £686 and £150 (remember that £150 per year would otherwise qualify the individual for the flat-rate pension, *if* he were a member of the scheme). For contracting out to be worthwhile it would therefore be necessary for the individual to join a private scheme which offers a ratio of annual pensions to annual contributions of 3·6. This value is obtained as the earnings-related component if he were in the state scheme (£1724–£910) divided by the contributions which could be transferred to a private scheme, £227. This ratio may be compared with the ratio of pensions to contributions for someone with earnings of £4000 but who is a full member of the scheme, which is £1724/£686 = 2·51. Without the imposition of differential contributions, the individual would obviously do much better simply by contracting out into a private scheme—even if that scheme only gave the same ratio of 2·51. His pension would be £910 + 2·51(£686 − £150) = £2255, which is higher than the £1724 given by the state scheme.

This section has shown the crucial nature of what have been called differential contributions to the state scheme by those who contract out, and which must be imposed for the state scheme to remain viable. It is also clear that contracting out must have implications for the levels of pensions which can be financed by total contributions. These implications are examined in the next section.

CONTRACTING OUT: EFFECTS ON COSTS

Proportional contributions with flat-rate pension

In order to examine the implications of contracting out for the alternative policy choices of benefits and contributions which are feasible, it is convenient to return to the simple framework introduced in chapter 3 which abstracts from the additional complications of earnings mobility and differential mortality. It is useful to consider first the scheme with directly proportional contributions combined with a flat-rate pension. Suppose further that individuals are allowed fully to contract out of the flat-rate pension and that this decision is not associated with a decision to save more for retirement. This last assumption avoids the considerable complications which would arise in attempting to combine a behavioural model of savings with the nature of individual incentives to contract out. Furthermore, and more importantly, the analysis is concerned exclusively with the question of whether to leave compulsory contributions in a state scheme or to invest in an alternative private scheme which yields a higher pension, without affecting the ability to consume during working life. It is therefore appropriate to consider the relative advantages of different schemes to individuals, where net income in working life remains unchanged. To abstract from the possible effects on capital markets of the number of people in private schemes it will also be assumed that individuals can invest privately at the same real rate of interest which is earned by the government pension fund. These assumptions make it possible to concentrate attention on the implications for various types of state scheme of alternative rules for contracting out.

Now the importance of the differential contributions to the state fund by those who contract out of the government pension has been discussed in the previous section. Suppose that in the present context such contributions are imposed by forcing individuals who contract out to continue to pay a proportion of their retirement savings into the fund, although they are not subsequently entitled to a state pension. The differential rate is directly measured by the proportional rate applied to contributions which would otherwise be paid into the government scheme. The effect of these contributions is to reduce the amount which the individual is able to transfer to a private scheme. This reduction is of course equivalent to a reduction in the rate of interest which may be obtained from the private investment. As stated in the previous section this effective reduction in the rate of interest is required in order to introduce stability into the state scheme, and to ensure that not everyone but the poorest individual will contract out. This may be seen as follows. Chart 3.4 of chapter 3 showed, for the simple framework used here, the way in which individuals with earnings greater than the arithmetic mean value of earnings obtain an implicit rate of return from the state scheme which is lower than the market rate of interest obtained by the pension fund. Now if all those above the arithmetic mean were to contract out of the state scheme without having to pay differential contributions, the amount available to distribute in flat-rate pensions would be correspondingly reduced. This would provide an incentive for a further group of individuals to contract out, and again the flat-rate pension would have to be reduced. Eventually no one would remain in the state scheme.

When differential contributions are imposed some individuals will be content to remain in the state scheme although they have an implicit rate of return which is less than the market rate of interest. This is because their implicit rate of return from the scheme is nevertheless higher than the effective rate of return which they could achieve by contracting out. An increase in the differential rate of contributions must increase the number of individuals who remain in the state scheme, and thereby increase the basic pension which the state fund is able to finance with any given proportional contributions rate.

The contracting out margin

The level of earnings above which it is worthwhile to contract out of the state scheme may be called the contracting out margin. All individuals with earnings below or equal to this margin will remain in the state scheme. At the contracting out margin the implicit rate of return obtained from the state scheme is equal to the rate of return which would be obtained by contracting out, when allowance is made for the existence of differential contributions. In the present case of a flat-rate pension combined with earnings-related contributions it can be shown that for a given distribution of annual earnings the contracting out margin depends *only* on the differential rate of contributions, and is independent of the market rate of interest and the contributions rate applying to those in the state scheme. Details are given in appendix A, but this convenient property means that the relationship can easily be shown diagrammatically.

Diagrammatic comparisons

The implications of this system of full contracting out of the flat-rate pension can conveniently be shown in chart 6.1. The horizontal axis of chart 6.1 shows the differential rate of contributions for those contracting out. For example, a differential rate of 0·2 means that each individual who contracts out must contribute 20 per cent of his retirement savings to the state fund, leaving 80 per cent to be invested at the same fixed rate of interest which is obtained by the state fund. In other words a person who is contracted out must contribute 20 per cent of the amount which someone with the same income, but in the state scheme, pays.

The vertical axis shows the level of earnings above which individuals have an incentive to contract out; what has been called the contracting out margin. The proportion of individuals involved may be obtained from details of the distribution of earnings shown in chart 3.1 of chapter 3. For example, when the differential rate is 0·2 the contracting-out margin is found to be £6000, which is 12 per cent higher than the arithmetic mean value of earnings. This in turn implies that 67 per cent of individuals remain in the state scheme. When the differential rate is increased to 0·35, then the contracting out margin is raised to £8000, and 86 per cent of the population remain in the state scheme. It is important to stress that these comparisons do not actually depend on the proportional rate of retirement savings (which is equal to the rate of contributions to the state scheme), or on the level of the flat-rate pension which is paid by the government scheme, or on the rate of interest. The derivation of these results is given in more detail in appendix A.

Having set the value of the differential rate of contributions and

Chart 6.1. *Contracting out: flat-rate pension*

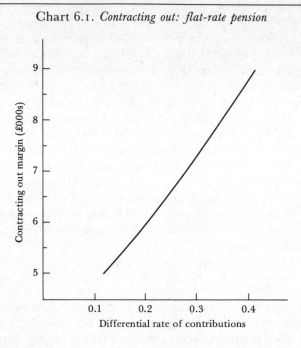

Chart 6.2. *Contributions and benefits*

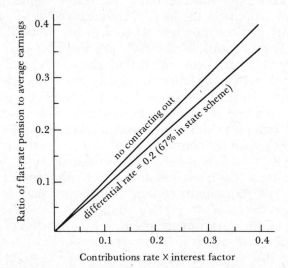

thereby determined the contracting out margin, it is possible to obtain the relationship between contributions and benefits for the state scheme, following the approach described in chapter 3. The introduction of the differential rate means that there is an additional policy variable to be chosen. Thus chart 6.2 shows the relationship between the flat-rate pension expressed as a proportion of average earnings and the product of the contributions rate and the interest factor. It can be seen that this relationship is a straight line, as in the corresponding system which does not allow contracting out. The example shown in chart 6.2 is for a differential rate of 0·2. The extent to which contracting out increases the contributions rate which is necessary to finance any given flat-rate pension is clearly shown by the fact that the relationship has a lower gradient than when contracting out is not permitted. The gradient is lower for a lower differential rate, since the contracting out margin is correspondingly lower.

A two-tier pension with partial contracting out

The same approach can then be used to examine the much more complex case which is closer to the new government scheme. Consider a system which has earnings-related contributions and a two-tier pension, and where individuals are allowed to contract out of the earnings-related tier, but still obtain the basic pension.[1] This system therefore allows partial contracting out, with a proportional reduction in the rate of contributions, as in the previous section. It should be noted that the system examined here, where those who are contracted out continue to pay an amount which is directly proportional to the contributions of someone in the state scheme with the same earnings, is slightly simpler than the new British scheme. As explained in the first section of this chapter, individuals who contract out of the British scheme pay the same contributions on earnings up to the value of the basic pension, and then pay a proportion of earnings measured above the basic pension. The British scheme therefore involves higher differential rates of contributions at all levels of earnings, but the variation in the differential rate with earnings is very similar for the two systems and the results presented here are therefore not sensitive to this assumption.[2]

When differential contributions are imposed there is again a level of earnings, the contracting out margin, at which the pension obtained in

---

[1] The scheme considered here, unlike the new state scheme, has no upper limit on contributions or benefits, but this aspect is discussed at the end of the third section.

[2] Individuals in the state scheme with earnings of y pay contributions of cy, and in the system examined in this section those who contract out pay contributions of δcy, implying a differential rate of contributions of $\delta \cdot b/y$. In the new British system it can be shown that differential contributions are equal to $\delta(1-b/y)$. The variation in the differential rate is considered again below.

the state scheme is exactly the same as that which could be obtained
by contracting out (and transferring the remaining contributions to a
private investment earning the same market rate of interest as the state
fund). In determining the contracting out margin allowance must of
course be made for the fact that the pension obtained from the state
scheme must vary as the proportion of people remaining in the state
scheme varies. Further details concerning the determination of this
margin are given in appendix A, where the relationship between the
contracting out margin and the proportion of retirement savings which
those individuals must continue to contribute to the state scheme, is
obtained. Remember that for the purpose of examining the incentive to
contract out, retirement savings in the present framework are determined simply as the contributions to the state scheme by someone who is
a full member.

Now in the earlier case of full contracting out of a flat-rate pension, the
proportion of savings which contracted out individuals have to pay to
the state scheme directly measured the differential rate of contributions.
The differential rate was therefore the same at all levels of earnings.
However, in the present case of partial contracting out it is very
important to realise that the proportional rate applied to those contracted out no longer measures the true differential rate of contributions.
This is simply because those individuals continue to receive a basic
pension.

The true differential rate is measured by the difference between the
compulsory contributions which must be made to the state scheme and
those which would otherwise be necessary to qualify for no more than
the basic pension within the state scheme, expressed as a proportion of
the contributions which would be made by someone with the same
income but in the state scheme. The differential rate therefore varies
systematically with earnings.

In order to illustrate this point it may be useful to refer to one of the
examples given in the discussion of the 1978 scheme in the first section of
this chapter. Table 6.1 shows that an individual earning £4000 per year
has to pay £686 if he is a member of the state scheme, but £459 if he is
contracted out. The annual contributions which would just qualify
someone for the basic pension are equal to £150. The differential rate of
contributions in this case is obtained as (£459–£150)/£686; that is 0·45.
An alternative way of describing the differential rate is to express it as
the proportion of retirement savings which are contributed to the state
scheme, less the ratio of the basic pension to the individual's annual
earnings. This clearly shows that the differential rate increases with
annual earnings, and it is this aspect which makes partial contracting
out more awkward to analyse.

The appropriate policy variable which must be chosen in the system of partial contracting out is of course the proportional rate which determines the proportion of an individual's contributions which must be left in the state scheme when he contracts out (what has also been referred to as the proportion of retirement savings contributed to the fund). This proportional rate does not *by itself* determine the schedule which relates differential rates of contributions to earnings, since that schedule also depends on the level of the basic pension which is paid to everyone (as shown in the previous paragraph). The policy decision does not therefore involve directly setting the differential rates. It requires a decision about only the *difference* in the contributions rate between those who are members and those who are contracted out of the state scheme.

The contracting out margin

It is therefore appropriate to examine first the relationship between the contracting out margin and the policy variables which directly affect it. In the previous case of full contracting out of a flat-rate pension it was found that the contracting out margin depended only on the choice of a single differential rate of contributions (as illustrated in chart 6.1). However, in the present more complex system the margin depends also on the basic minimum pension and on the proportional pension rate which is used in the second tier. Chart 6.3 therefore illustrates the relationship between the contracting out margin and the proportion of retirement savings required from those contracted out, for two values of the basic pension and three proportional pension rates.

Chart 6.3 clearly shows that the schedules are further to the right, implying higher proportional rates, as the basic pension is increased, and as the proportional pension rate of the upper tier is reduced. These general results are to be expected from the previous analysis of chapter 3. However, an interesting and unexpected feature of chart 6.3 is that for each combination of values of the basic pension and the proportional pension rate, an increase in the proportion of retirement savings which must be contributed to the fund by those contracted out (on the horizontal axis) is no longer always associated with an increase in the proportion of individuals who remain in the state scheme (indicated by a movement up the vertical axis). The range of values for which the opposite is true is greater as the proportional pension rate increases. This property is most clearly shown by a comparison of curve E for a pension rate of 5 per cent of earnings in excess of the basic minimum with curve B for a pension rate of 20 per cent, both with a basic pension of 22 per cent of average earnings. The important implication of this property for government policy is that there is no longer a unique functional relationship between the contracting out margin and the

Chart 6.3. *Contracting out of the two-tier pension*

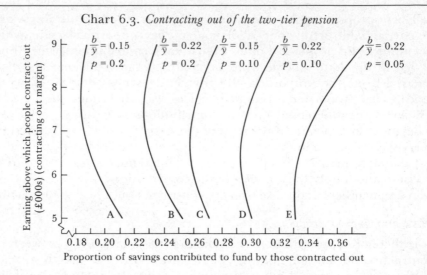

Proportion of savings contributed to fund by those contracted out

policy variable (the proportion of savings which must be contributed to the fund by those contracted out). There is more than one value of the former corresponding to any given value of the latter!

It is important to realise when considering chart 6.3 that changes in the rate at which retirement savings must be contributed to the state fund, by those contracted out, will also be accompanied by changes in the actual amount saved out of any given income. Thus a movement along any of the curves in chart 6.3 (for which the basic pension and proportional pension rate is held constant) must also imply a change in the contributions rate for those who are full members of the state scheme. The change is necessary in order to continue paying the same pensions while the number of individuls contracting out of the scheme varies. And it is this contributions rate which determines the savings rate of those contracted out, in the context of the framework used here.

Differential rate of contributions

Having obtained the relationships in chart 6.3 it is now possible to consider how the differential rate of contributions varies. It has already been stressed that the differential rate depends on the individual's level of earnings, so that the most useful comparisons are between different rates at the contracting out margin; that is, for the income at which an individual will be indifferent towards either contracting out or remaining in the state scheme. Consider then curve A in chart 6 where the basic pension is 15 per cent of average earnings and the proportional pension rate is 20 per cent of earnings in excess of the basic minimum. Using the definition of the differential rate given in the previous section, it is found that the value of the rate for a contracting out margin of £5000 is 0·052; that is 0·212 − (800/5000). Thus for an individual at the margin, 5·2 per cent of his savings must be contributed to the state scheme although they do not subsequently entitle that individual to an earnings-related pension. For contracting out margins of £6000, £7000, £8000 and £9000 the differential rates must be 0·062, 0·071, 0·083 and 0·098 respectively. An increase in the number of individuals remaining within the state scheme is associated with an increase, at the contracting out margin, in the differential rate of contributions to the state scheme which applies to those who contract out.

This result must of course necessarily hold, but as shown above, a fundamental difficulty with this system is raised by the fact that the differential rates (more precisely, the schedule relating the differential rates to earnings) do not result from setting a single policy variable. In addition to the basic pension, the relevant policy variable is actually the (proportional) difference between the contributions rate for those in the system and the contributions rate for those contracted out. As clearly shown in chart 6.3, a decrease in that difference may in some circumstances lead to a decrease in the number of individuals who are contracted out of the state scheme, and vice versa. This perverse response to one of the available policy variables must inevitably lead to difficulties in pension administration.

Contributions and benefits

The effect of partial contracting out of the two-tier pension scheme on the contributions required to finance alternative benefits can be seen in chart 6.4 which shows the relationship between the basic pension as a proportion of average earnings and the product of the contributions rate and the interest factor, for a proportional pension rate of 20 per cent. The corresponding relationship where individuals cannot contract out (taken from chapter 3) is also shown in chart 6.4 for comparison.

It is of interest to note that the relationship is again given by a straight line, and the extent to which the achievement of any given basic pension requires a much higher rate of contributions as more people contract out of the second tier is also evident. A comparison between chart 6.4 and chart 6.2 clearly shows the greater effect on the relationship between contributions and benefits of partial contracting out of a two-tier pension compared with the effect of full contracting out of a flat-rate pension. Not only are higher contributions required to achieve any given basic pension in the two-tier system, but with contracting out it becomes relatively more difficult to increase the basic pension.

Consider, for example, the flat-rate scheme for which it is required to have a basic minimum pension of 20 per cent of average earnings. A

Chart 6.4. *Contributions and benefits*

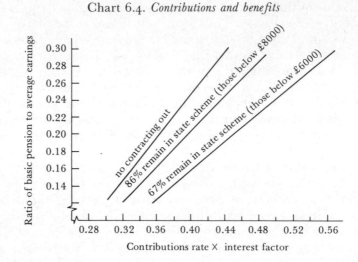

Note: Earnings-related proportion = 0·2.

change from compulsory full membership of the scheme to contracting out, with differential rates such that 67 per cent of the population remain in the state scheme, will require the contributions rate to be increased by $12\frac{1}{2}$ per cent. The corresponding increase for partial contracting out of a two-tier pension scheme, where the earnings-related proportion used in the upper tier of the pension is 0·2, is almost double, at 23·8 per cent.

It has therefore been seen that, even in the context of a very simple model, the desire to have a state pension scheme with both an earnings-related tier and partial contracting out introduces considerable complexities. Policy decisions about appropriate rates of contributions and benefits become very much more difficult than in systems without either contracting out or earnings-related tiers. It has sometimes been claimed, furthermore, that the imposition of differential contributions on those who contract out of state schemes makes it possible to continue any redistribution which may be involved in the state scheme. This issue is considered in the following section.

CONTRACTING OUT: EFFECTS ON REDISTRIBUTION

This section examines the effects on redistribution of contracting out of both the flat-rate and two-tier pension schemes which were considered in the previous section. The extent to which the results may be modified by earnings mobility and differential mortality have not been examined using the simulations which have been discussed in chapters 4 and 5. It is, however, immediately clear from the results presented in chapter 5 that differential mortality reduces the extent of redistribution which is implied by the present simplified model. The introduction of earnings mobility would raise a further number of complex behavioural problems, since it would be necessary to consider precisely how individuals form and revise expectations about their future earnings. It would also give rise to the possibility of people regretting a decision to contract out. Furthermore, the notion of a contracting out margin, such that all individuals with earnings above that margin have an incentive to contract out of the state scheme, no longer becomes appropriate. This is because with earnings mobility the decision to contract out will depend on the complete time profile of earnings and on the nature of expectations. For these reasons it seems most useful to compare alternative schemes within the very simple framework used in this chapter, and first outlined in chapter 3.

Proportional contributions and flat-rate pension

Consider first the effect on the dispersion of the discounted value of net lifetime income, of full contracting out of a scheme with a flat-rate pension and proportional contributions. The method of analysis proceeds as described in chapter 5 (second section) and in this case it is of course necessary to divide the population into two groups, separated by the contracting out margin. Details of the calculations are given in appendix A, and examples are shown in chart 6.5 for two alternative proportional contribution rates of 0·1 and 0·2. The vertical axis shows the value of the coefficient of variation of net lifetime income, and the horizontal axis shows the level of earnings above which individuals contract out of the scheme; that is, the contracting out margin. As explained in the previous section, the contracting out margin can be increased by increasing the single differential rate of contributions to the state scheme by those contracted out (see chart 6.1). Chart 6.5 shows how the coefficient of variation of net lifetime income varies with the contracting out margin, for two rates of proportional contributions, 10 per cent and 20 per cent. This is indicated by the lines marked AB and CD respectively. The relationship for the former rate is obviously above that of the latter rate, since the higher contributions of CD enable a higher flat-rate pension to be paid, and hence make for lower dispersion.

The two horizontal lines in chart 6.5 show the value of the coefficient of variation for corresponding schemes which do not allow contracting out. The further to the right, along the lines AB and CD, the closer is the scheme to the one which does not allow contracting out, since each downward sloping line asymptotically approaches its corresponding

Chart 6.5. *Dispersion of net lifetime income: flat-rate pension*

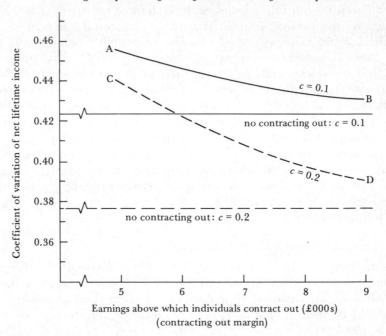

Earnings above which individuals contract out (£000s)
(contracting out margin)

c = proportional rate of contributions for those contracted into state system

horizontal line. The intercept of both AB and CD on the vertical axis is of course 0·471, the coefficient of variation of earnings during the working period, since at that point the contracting out margin is zero and the state scheme is non-existent.

It should be noted that within this kind of scheme the coefficient of variation of discounted net income, for given values of the contributions rate and the differential rate, does not depend on the interest factor. Nevertheless the level of the flat-rate pension received by those remaining in the state scheme will obviously depend on the value of the interest factor and on the proportion of individuals who contract out of the scheme, as has been shown in chart 6.2.

Two-tier pension with partial contracting out

The case of a two-tier state pension where individuals are allowed to contract out of the earnings-related pension is shown in chart 6.6. Examples here are all given for an interest factor of 1·6.[1] However, in

---

[1] The population must be divided into three groups: those with earnings below the basic pension; those between the basic pension and the contracting out margin; and those above the latter margin.

Chart 6.6. *Dispersion of net lifetime income: two-tier pension*

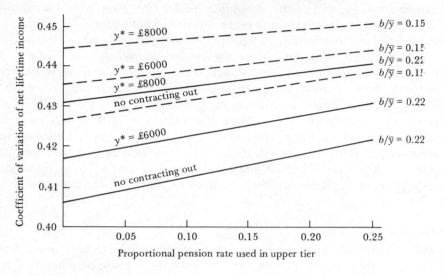

Note: Interest factor = 1·6.

KEY

y^* = threshold level of annual earnings above which individuals contract out (contracting out margin)

$b/\bar{y}$ = ratio of basic minimum pension to average annual earnings ($\bar{y}$ = £5431)

making comparisons it should always be remembered that the contributions rate required to finance any given basic pension in the two-tier scheme is increased as more individuals contract out of the scheme, as has been indicated in chart 6.4. Results are shown in table 6.6 for two ratios of the basic pension to average earnings and for two different levels of the contracting out margin. Comparisons are also shown for a two-tier scheme which has the same pensions but does not allow contracting out. It can be seen that the relationship between the proportional pension rate used in the upper tier of the pension and the dispersion of discounted net life income is in each case given by a straight line. The intercept on the horizontal axis is of course the coefficient of variation in a scheme which has only a basic pension.

Examination of chart 6.6 clearly shows that the ability partially to contract out of the two-tier pension significantly affects the redistributive nature of the pension scheme, although some intra-generational redistribution does take place. However, the simulation results of the third section of chapter 5 are again worth considering at this point. It was shown, for schemes without contracting out, that allowance for earnings mobility and differential mortality meant that there was an insignificant amount of systematic redistribution. This was true even where the earlier analysis, within the simplified model also used here, had shown that the scheme implied some redistribution. Furthermore the scheme in chart 6.6 does not contain an upper limit on pensions and contributions; a feature which, as has been shown in chapter 5, also limits the redistributive element of pension schemes. The present framework does not seem well suited to the treatment of contracting out where there are upper limits on annual contributions and benefits. For example, it would be expected that all those above the earnings limit would have an incentive to contract out. However, implications of upper limits for the relationship between contributions and benefits (as in chart 3.3) are relevant here, so that the maintenance of a given basic minimum requires even higher contributions than indicated in chart 6.4.

CONCLUSIONS

This chapter has examined some implications of the facility to contract out of a state pension scheme, for both feasible levels of pensions and the possible lifetime redistribution implied by various schemes. It is obvious that any system which involves systematic redistribution will provide an incentive for the higher earners to leave the state scheme and transfer their contributions, or life cycle savings, to a private scheme which is more closely governed by actuarial considerations. If individuals are entirely free to contract out of the state scheme without contracting to contribute to the state fund, then there is obviously less available to redistribute to the lower earners, and the pensions of those remaining in the state scheme must be reduced. This will have the effect of introducing a further group of individuals who would benefit from contracting out, and the system would ultimately be unstable with only those who cannot find a private pension scheme remaining in the state scheme.

The basis of contracting-out arrangements is therefore that differential contributions must be levied on those who contract out, thereby reducing the effective market rate of interest which they can obtain. Despite the imposition of high differential rates the results of this chapter have shown that contracting out imposes severe contraints on the ability to maintain a reasonable level of the basic minimum pension. This is particularly true of partial contracting out of two-tier pension schemes, where it has been shown that policy choices of contribution and benefit levels are much more difficult because of the problem of estimating the proportion of the population who are likely to leave the state system. Furthermore, the redistributive ability of any scheme is considerably reduced when contracting out is allowed.

7

NATIONAL INSURANCE POLICY

SUMMARY OF RESULTS

As outlined in chapter 1, the purpose of this book has been to examine a limited number of aspects of state pensions in Britain, with particular reference to the new state scheme which was introduced in 1978. The new British scheme is probably the most complex pension scheme in the world, and involved the introduction of a number of novel departures from previous experience, whose implications are difficult to predict. During the middle and late 1970s the British economy experienced relatively large changes in unemployment, and in the rate of increase in retail prices and average earnings. The increased uncertainty resulting from these rapid changes, combined with the considerable complexity of the system, makes the task of estimating the financial implications of the scheme extremely difficult. The significant problems of predicting demographic changes, and changes in labour force participation, especially of married women, should also not be forgotten.[1] As if these problems were not enough, the state pension system interacts in an extremely complex way with the private pension industry, the systems of income and corporation tax, and the Supplementary Benefit system. A comprehensive analysis of pensions would therefore require the resources of a large multi-disciplinary research team, with access to a large amount of data which are not yet available.

It is therefore *not* the purpose of this book to criticise, for example, the work of the Government Actuary's Department, which is in the unenviable position of being required to produce independent estimates while receiving specific instructions about its assumptions relating to some of the crucial variables, such as the rates of inflation and of unemployment. This study has examined only a small number of aspects of state pension schemes, namely some of the more novel aspects of the new scheme which have necessarily been given little attention in the past. Indeed, in the course of the analysis it has been necessary to abstract from a very large number of the complexities which cannot be ignored by the Government Actuary in producing his estimates. It is nevertheless

---

[1] For an interesting analysis of demographic factors see J. Ermisch, 'Implications of demographic developments for the state pension scheme', *Pensions World*, vol. 10, no. 3, March 1981.

hoped that concentration on these issues has helped to clarify some difficulties which may have sometimes confused the choice between alternative schemes.

The analysis of each chapter was concerned with a single cohort of individuals, and consistently took a lifetime perspective. It may also be worth repeating here that the formal model of pensions used throughout the study, except in the simulation exercise of chapter 4, was in the context of a funded scheme, where pensions were financed fully from the contributions of the cohort, although the same contributions and pension rates applied to all individuals (there is of course no screening or individual risk rating in the state pension scheme). This kind of framework, while obviously an abstraction from reality, is necessary when considering the relationship between pensions and contributions in different types of scheme, and when examining lifetime intra-generational redistribution. If each generation's pensions were not assumed to be funded from special contributions, it would then have been necessary to examine the implications of alternative methods of finance.

Earnings-related benefits

It has been seen that in the development of the present system there has been some conflict between the objectives of income replacement and of preventing poverty in old age. Although initially there was greater emphasis on preventing poverty, while also attempting to avoid some of the difficulties associated with the operation of the Poor Law and the means-test, in recent years there has been greater emphasis on income replacement. There has also been considerable growth in the means-tested sector. The recent emphasis which has led to earnings-related benefits has to some extent been associated with what has been referred to as the insurance myth, but the specific official arguments have not usually been made explicit. But as one study recently argued, poverty prevention, 'may indeed suffer to some extent if attention is mainly concentrated on the replacement of unequal incomes by unequal pensions after retirement'.[1]

It is of course most important to stress that the final decision will depend on political judgement about the desirability of redistribution, as well as on considerations of administrative efficiency, and on possible incentive effects.[2] One main objective of this study has been to attempt to make explicit the nature of the trade-offs involved in moving from one

---

[1] See Wilson (ed.), *Pensions, Inflation and Growth*, p. 27.
[2] Of course, it cannot be expected that the precise arguments will be explicit, or will be made explicit in policy announcements. An example is provided by the recent plan to abolish earnings-related supplement for the eligible unemployed.

type of scheme to another. The extent to which different policies represent consistent aims can therefore also be seen.

Now it may be felt by the policy maker that the main purpose of a pension scheme is to provide suitable income replacement in old age, and that individuals will not make the appropriate decisions relating to savings over their working life. This may be either because of a lack of foresight, or because they do not have access to the kind of information necessary to make useful decisions—including information about future government policy—or because it is extremely expensive to collect the information and a great deal of skill is required to make appropriate judgements. The same policy maker may feel that poverty prevention is best dealt with by other methods of income transfer, and that the aged poor should be helped in just the same kind of way as other groups of deserving poor. Such arguments will lead to the suggestion that there should be a compulsory system of earnings-related state insurance, financed from a special hypothecated tax (such as National Insurance contributions); the fact that such a system cannot easily pay a high basic pension—as shown in chapter 3—will be of little concern. But to propose that individuals should then be able partially to contract out of the state scheme, to join a private scheme, requires further argument for its support. To further suggest that contracted out individuals should receive special tax advantages requires even more specific detailed support.[1] If, for example, it is thought to be more efficient for the state to administer an earnings-related scheme (efficiency in information collection, in decision making and record keeping), then the support of partial contracting out must appeal to a different kind of argument. The arguments for the very strong support for the private pension industry which is provided by the present state scheme have not been made explicit, however.

It has also been shown in chapter 6 that partial contracting out of an earnings-related state pension is likely to lead to significant administrative difficulties relating to the decisions concerning appropriate contributions rates for those in the scheme, and the need to set reduced rates for those contracted out. Also, higher contributions rates are required to

---

[1] Included in such advantages are the favourable tax treatment of pension funds, the fact that superannuation contributions count as eligible allowances for purposes of income taxation, and the fact that private schemes will be supported from general exchequer funds. The issue of the tax treatment of pension contributions is of course related to the well known problems of double taxation, and differentiation of income tax according to the source of income. (For discussion and references see F. Shehab, *Progressive Taxation*, Oxford University Press, 1953, pp. 92–4, 107–11.) The present system obviously does not reflect a consistent view about double taxation. Notice also that proposals to tax National Insurance benefits along with other income (where contributions are not offset against income for tax purposes) necessarily involves regarding the system simply as a tax-transfer mechanism, and eschewing the mythical idea of insurance.

maintain the same replacement rates as in a scheme without contracting out.

Furthermore, the usual arguments in favour of state earnings-related pensions do not directly support a scheme in which an individual who has contributed for only twenty years may receive a pension equal to that of someone who has contributed for over 45 years—as in the current scheme based on the best twenty years' earnings.

One interpretation of the present system is that it seems to reflect a significant amount of inconsistency—especially when it is recalled that some supporters of the new scheme have actually claimed the alleviation of poverty in old age as one of the scheme's main objectives and merits.[1] The most reasonable interpretation of this inconsistency is that the scheme reflects a considerable amount of compromise which was undoubtedly necessary in order to obtain agreement from so many different parties (after several occasions when a scheme was aborted by an incoming government following a general election). This also explains, to some extent at least, the considerable complexity of the new scheme, so that many policy makers cannot be expected to appreciate fully the implications of their decisions.

If, however, the policy maker feels that a major purpose of pensions should be to prevent poverty in old age, and to be an instrument for the redistribution of lifetime income, then the results presented in this study suggest that a decision should be made in favour of flat-rate pensions financed from earnings-related contributions. Individuals would be able to join private schemes if they wished to supplement the flat-rate pension, but the policy maker would be unlikely to support full contracting out or generous tax subsidies to the private pension industry. While flat-rate pensions would provide a considerable simplification, when compared with the present scheme, and also enable large administrative savings to be made, it must not be thought that all difficult pension issues would be avoided.[2] The maintenance of any given level of pensions, for example relative to average earnings, depends crucially on what happens to productivity and population growth. It would also be necessary to decide which individuals will be eligible for full pension rights, and how the system would interact with the supplementary benefit and income taxation systems.

[1] See, for example, Atkinson, 'The developing relationship between the state pension scheme and occupational pension schemes', p. 216, and the discussion by J. Stern in D. Collard, J. R. Lecomber and M. Slater (eds.), *Income Distribution; the Limits to Redistribution*, Bristol, Scientechnica, 1980, p. 120.

[2] When commenting on proposals for flat-rate benefits A. R. Prest wrote, 'This seems to me totally unrealistic. Short term earnings-related benefits are now a well-established fact of life in this country, as in others' ('The structure and reform of direct taxation', *Economic Journal*, vol. 89, 1979, p. 251). But less than one year later the Conservative government proposed to abolish earnings-related unemployment benefits!

INTEGRATION OF NATIONAL INSURANCE AND TAXATION

There has in fact been a significant amount of pressure for flat-rate pensions (and other insurance benefits), and for the taxation of benefits in line with other sources of income.[1]

If it is also accepted that National Insurance contributions and benefits bear no relation to an insurance scheme, and that a major rationale for the existence of such benefits is precisely that it should *not* behave like an insurance system (which would not cover high risk people), then the suggestion that it should be integrated into a general system of taxation and social security naturally arises. The imposition of an employers' surcharge on National Insurance contributions, which is paid directly into general exchequer funds, is also highly anomalous. It is sometimes argued that people think that insurance contributions are in some sense different from income taxation, and will therefore be willing to pay more, but this kind of argument could surely not be maintained for long. As one observer has commented,

If part is not recognised to be a tax at all, but regarded more benignly as a Social Insurance contribution, then taxpayers may still be willing to carry a heavy total burden—although this is not, perhaps, a point that could be securely defended on grounds of social ethics.[2]

It may be suggested, however, that while most people regard their National Insurance contributions as a form of direct taxation, the complexity of the system ensures that it is extremely difficult (if not impossible) to know how the burden of taxation is distributed or what integration of the systems would imply for the overall tax rate. Although it is more appropriate to regard insurance contributions as a form of taxation, it is certainly a rather strange kind of tax under the present set of regulations.

Individuals do not become liable to National Insurance contributions until a lower earnings limit has been reached, after which contributions are a constant proportion of gross earnings up to a maximum. The marginal rate of contributions at the lower limit is therefore very high, while it is zero after the upper limit has been exceeded. Notice that this is quite different from normal income taxation, which is based on income in excess of the value of eligible allowances. Those who are contracted out of the earnings-related pension pay the full contribution rate on earnings up to the lower limit, and then pay a reduced rate on earnings between the lower and upper limits. Contributions to the contracted out

[1] See, for example, J. E. Meade *et al*, *The Structure and Reform of Direct Taxation*, London, Allen & Unwin, 1978.
[2] Wilson (ed.), *Pensions, Inflation and Growth*, p. 16.

scheme are subtracted from gross income before taxable income is calculated, but the National Insurance contributions are not deductible. It is difficult to see any justification for either the high marginal rates at the lower limit, or for the different treatment of superannuation contributions for tax purposes; what amounts to discrimination in favour of those contributing to contracted out schemes.

National Insurance contributions are based on weekly earnings (or monthly earnings, depending on the period of payment) with no provision for averaging over the financial year as in the income tax. This difference in the period of assessments is rather arbitrary, and mainly affects those whose earnings fluctuate around the upper limit from week to week. This is also significant in recent years where large sums have been paid in back-dated pay covering a number of months. Because of the upper limit and the fact that earnings are not averaged over the period of back payment, National Insurance contributions are lower than they would be if the pay increases had actually begun at the earlier date.

Although the integration of National Insurance contributions with income taxation has been suggested by a number of authors, the implications for revenue have been given surprisingly little attention. If, for simplicity, income tax is regarded as being a constant proportion of income above the level of eligible allowances, then the tax rate required in an integrated system in order to raise the same total revenue is not simply equal to the sum of the previous tax and contributions rates. This is because of the difference between the lower limit relating to contributions and the relevant tax allowances, and especially the fact that contributions are proportional to gross earnings. Integration involves a loss of revenue for these reasons which is greater than the gain in revenue resulting from the abolition of the upper earnings limit on contributions. Results presented in appendix C suggest that for current rates of contributions the integrated tax rate may need to be greater than the sum of the two separate rates by as much as 5 percentage points. This result must not of course be thought to support the view that taxable capacity is increased by the use of a number of separate taxes, as the comparison is between systems with the same total revenue.

It is also important to note that a change to an integrated system involves a quite different distribution of the burden of taxation. In particular it would eliminate the high marginal rate at the lower earnings limit for contributions, and the zero marginal rate above the upper limit. It is therefore not necessarily appropriate to compare systems which raise the same total revenue, since they involve different distributions of post-tax income. The integrated system is of course more generous to those in the middle income range, between the contributions limits, and in considering the details of any change the desired amount of redistribution would have to be specified explicitly.

It must be stressed that the suggestion that National Insurance should be integrated with income taxation does not necessarily imply that there should be no partial pension fund. Indeed, as argued in chapter 2, variations in anticipated payments due to demographic and other factors are usefully met by a fund; and of course the present system is run largely on a pay-as-you-go basis along with a small fund.

To suggest that benefits should be flat-rate, rather than earnings-related, still leaves unanswered many difficult questions associated with the administration of benefits (and especially of unemployment benefits). These problems concern the coverage of and eligibility for benefits, the time period of payment, and the treatment of dependants. As noted earlier there has been a recent significant shift towards means-testing, despite the problems which have been extensively discussed elsewhere (including administrative inefficiency, low take-up, and problems of coordinating many different benefits to avoid marginal tax rates exceeding 100 per cent).

Income taxation is of course a special type of means-test, but the granting of an unconditional benefit which is then subject to taxation along with other income is a very different system from one in which certain benefits are granted only after close scrutiny of certain means by Supplementary Benefit officials. The two types of means-testing represent asymmetric methods of dealing with individuals, their needs and resources; they are not simple administrative alternatives.

Returning to the opening sentence of this book, it seems that after almost a lifetime of experience during two world wars and considerable variations in economic conditions, the great liberal 'brainchild' of National Insurance may well be laid to rest. But it must be remembered that the death of its aged predecessor the old Poor Law took a long and painful time.

APPENDIX A

SOME ANALYTICS OF PENSION SCHEMES

The purpose of this appendix is to provide some details of the pension schemes discussed in chapters 3, 4 and 6. In each case a simple framework of analysis was used which abstracted from the problems raised by earnings variability over the working life and by differential mortality. These latter problems were examined using a simulation analysis, and the details of the simulation model are given in appendix B.

As explained in chapter 3, the analytical results apply to a single cohort of individuals, each member of which lives and works for the same number of years, and receives a constant stream of earnings. This simplification enables the analysis to proceed as if life were divided into two periods of work and retirement, and each of earnings, contributions and pensions for each individual can be consolidated into a single figure. The total contributions to the fund are increased by a single interest payment.

The following notation is used consistently in this appendix.

N = Number of individuals in the cohort
y_i = earnings of individual i over the working period
$\bar{y}$ = arithmetic mean lifetime earnings (over the first period) of individuals in the cohort
$C(y_i)$ = total contributions of the ith individual to the state pension fund
$P(y_i)$ = total pension received by the ith individual in the retirement period
r = rate of interest, so that the interest factor is equal to $1 + r$
z_i = individual i's total discounted net income
$= y_i - C(y_i) + \{P(y_i)/(1 + r)\}$
c = proportional rate of contributions to state pension fund
p = proportional pension rate
b = basic minimum pension over the second or retirement period
m = upper limit on earnings, for contributions and pensions

Consider first the case of directly proportional contributions and pensions, where $P(y_i) = py_i$ and $C(y_i) = cy_i$. The total contributions of $Nc\bar{y}$ are placed in an interest earning fund which in turn must finance total pensions of $N p \bar{y}$. This means that $N c(1 + r) \bar{y}$ must be equal to $N p \bar{y}$ for the scheme to be self financing, so that $p = c(1 + r)$. This provides a simple relationship between the two proportional rates.

The total discounted net income of the ith individual, denoted by z_i, is his lifetime earnings, y_i, minus his total contributions $C(y_i)$, plus the discounted value of his total pension receipts, $P(y_i)/(1 + r)$. Now in the case of proportional contributions and benefits it is easily seen that $z_i = y_i$, since $p = c(1 + r)$ and thus the relative dispersion of z is the same as that of y. Hence the scheme does not involve any intra-generational redistribution. This basic method of analysis can then be applied to more complex schemes.[1] If proportional contributions are used to finance a flat-rate pension then total pension payments are simply Nb, and when this is equated to accumulated contributions $N \bar{y} c(1 + r)$ it is easily seen that $b/\bar{y} = c(1 + r)$. Here c and r determine the ratio of the flat-rate pension to arithmetic mean earnings. This is shown by the 45° line in chart 3.2 of chapter 3.

Two-tier pension with proportional contributions

Proportional contributions may be combined with a two-tier pension of the following type

$$P(y) = b \qquad\qquad y \leqslant b$$
$$ = b + p(y - b) \; y > b \qquad\qquad (1)$$

In this case the amount needed to finance pensions at the basic rate is simply Nb, and the pension payments on incomes above b are equal to $N p \int_b (y - b) dF(y)$. Here $F(y)$ denotes the distribution function of income, and gives the proportion of individuals with income less than or equal to any given value of y. Total pension payments are therefore

$$Nb + Np \int_b (y - b) dF(y) \qquad\qquad (2)$$

The expression in (2) can be rearranged to give

$$Nb + Np[\bar{y}\{1 - F_1(b)\} - b\{1 - F(b)\}]$$

where $F_1(y)$ denotes the proportion of total income accounted for by all those individuals with incomes not exceeding y. $F_1(y)$ is called the first moment distribution of income, and is defined by $F_1(y) = (1/\bar{y}) \int^y u \, dF(u)$. If the function $h(y)$ is defined as

$$h(y) = F_1(y) + y\{1 - F(y)\}/\bar{y} \qquad\qquad (3)$$

---

[1] Some further applications of this model are discussed in J. Creedy, 'Pension Schemes and the limits to redistribution', in Collard, Lecomber and Slater (eds.), *Income distribution; the Limits to Redistribution*.

then total pension payments can be more conveniently expressed as

$$\bar{y}N[(b/\bar{y}) + p\{1 - h(b)\}] \tag{4}$$

In fact the function $h(y)$ measures the proportion of total income obtained by those with not more than y, plus the product of the proportion of the population earning at least y, and the ratio of y to arithmetic mean earnings.

In this system there are three policy variables, c, p and b, although only two variables may be chosen independently since the expression in (4) must be equated to total accumulated contributions, which as before is equal to $Nc(1 + r)\bar{y}$. For the computations reported in chapter 3 it is most convenient to set b and p, and then to determine $(1 + r)c$. The comparisons are shown in chart 3.2. The need to use the first moment distribution also indicates why the lognormal distribution of income is so useful in this context, since its moment distributions are easily obtained from the distribution function. If income is distributed lognormally as $\Lambda(y \mid \mu, \sigma^2)$, where μ and σ^2 are respectively the mean and variance of the logarithms of income, then the jth moment distribution is given as

$$\Lambda_j(y \mid \mu, \sigma^2) = \Lambda(y \mid \mu + j\sigma^2, \sigma^2) \tag{5}$$

where by definition $\Lambda_j(y) = \int^y u^j F(u) / \int u^j dF(u)$.[1]

As noted in chapter 3, the values of μ and σ^2 were set at $8 \cdot 5$ and $0 \cdot 2$ respectively, implying an arithmetic mean and coefficient of variation of y of £5431 and $0 \cdot 471$ respectively. These values roughly apply to average lifetime earnings in 1973 prices. The distribution function $F(y)$, and the Lorenz curve (which shows the relationship between $F(y)$ and $F_1(y)$, the proportion of individuals obtaining a certain proportion of total income) are both illustrated in chart 3.1.

Two-tier pension with upper earnings limits

The pension scheme introduced in Great Britain in 1978 is similar to this two-tier scheme, except that there is an upper limit to earnings, beyond which no contributions are paid or earnings-related pension received. Thus

$$\begin{aligned} P(y) &= b & y \leq b \\ &= b + p(y - b) & b < y \leq m \\ &= b + p(m - b) & y > m \end{aligned} \tag{6}$$

Although there is the additional policy variable m, an additional constraint is imposed by the requirement that $m = 7b$.

The calculation of total contributions to this scheme is obviously complicated by the upper limit; the contributions of all those below the

---

[1] See Aitchison and Brown, *The Lognormal Distribution*, p. 12.

limit depends on their total income (given by the first moment distribution) while the contributions of those with incomes above the limit depends on the number of those individuals (given by the distribution function). It is not possible to reproduce here all the stages in the derivation, but after some manipulation it is found that total accumulated contributions are equal to

$$N c \bar{y} (1 + r) h(m) \tag{7}$$

where the function $h(.)$ is that defined in equation (3) above. Total pension payments, after some manipulation, are found to be equal to

$$N \bar{y} [(b/\bar{y}) \{2 - F(m)\} + p \{h(m) - h(b)\}] \tag{8}$$

By combining equations (7) and (8) it is possible to calculate the value of $(1 + r)c$ corresponding to any given values of p and b (and therefore m, since $m = 7b$). This method is used to obtain chart 3.3, of chapter 3.

Dispersion of total net income

Consider first the case of proportional contributions with a flat-rate pension. Here there is a simple relationship between z and y for each individual, since $z = y - C(y) + P(y)/(1 + r) = y(1 - c) + c\bar{y}$. There is therefore a simple linear transformation between the distributions of z and of y. Now in the general case of a linear transformation where $z = \xi y + \psi$, it can easily be seen that $E(z) = \xi E(y) + \psi$ and $V(z) = \xi^2 V(y)$; where E and V denote 'expected value' and 'variance' respectively. Thus if η_y and η_z are used to denote the coefficient of variation of the two distributions of y and z respectively, it can be shown that $\eta_z = \eta_y \{1 + \psi/\xi E(y)\}^{-1}$. Substitution of $c\bar{y}$ for ψ and $(1 - c)$ for ξ in this context therefore gives the result that $\eta_z = (1 - c)\eta_y$, so that the redistributive effect of this scheme can easily be obtained.

The redistributive effect of two-tier schemes is, however, more difficult to calculate. Where there is no upper earnings limit the population is divided into two sections according to whether earnings are above or below the basic pension. The linear transformations between y and total net discounted income in the two groups are given by

$$z = y(1 - c) + b/(1 + r) \qquad\qquad y \le b$$

and $\quad z = y(1 - c) + \{b + p(y - b)\}/(1 + r) \qquad y > b \tag{9}$
$$= y\{(1 - c) + p/(1 + r)\} + b(1 - p)/(1 + r)$$

It is therefore necessary to consider the dispersion of net income within each group separately, and then to combine the groups in a suitable way. This need to decompose the population dispersion into separate groups, combined with the need to have a convenient transformation between the dispersion of z and y within each group, explains why the coefficient of variation is used as a measure of dispersion, since it is the most tractable measure.

For convenience of exposition, suppose that the population is divided into two groups as follows

$$z = \xi_1 y + \psi_1 \qquad y < y^* \\ = \xi_2 y + \psi_2 \qquad y > y^* \tag{10}$$

Further, write $E_1(z)$ for $E(z \mid y < y^*)$ and $V_1(z)$ for $V(z \mid y < y^*)$, which are respectively the arithmetic mean and variance of the lower part of the sample. Similar definitions apply to $E_2(z)$ and $V_2(z)$ for those with incomes above y^*. Furthermore, the proportion of the population below and above the value of y^*, $F(y^*)$ and $1 - F(y^*)$, may be written as w_1 and w_2 respectively. The population mean and variance, $E(z)$ and $V(z)$ respectively, are given by

$$E(z) = w_1 E_1(z) + w_2 E_2(z) \\ V(z) = w_1 V_1(z) + w_2 V_2(z) + w_1 w_2 \{E_1(z) - E_2(z)\}^2 \tag{11}$$

The value of η_z can then easily be obtained as $V(z)^{\frac{1}{2}} / E(z)$.

It remains to derive expressions for the calculation of the means and variances of the sub-samples, for substitution into equations (11) above. The most convenient expressions from the point of view of the calculations are

$$E_1(z) = \xi_1 \bar{y} F_1(y^*) / w_1 + \psi_1 \tag{12}$$

$$V_1(z) = \xi_1^2 \{V(y) + \bar{y}^2\} F_2(y^*) / w_1 - \{\xi_1 y F_1(y^*) / w_1\}^2 \tag{13}$$

where $V(y)$ is the variance of y and $F_2(y)$ denotes the second moment distribution of income. The corresponding values of $E_2(z)$ and $V_2(z)$ can be obtained from equations (11) and (12) by substituting ξ_2 for ξ_1, ψ_2 for ψ_1 and w_2 for w_1.

The case of a two-tier pension with an upper limit introduces the additional complication of a third group; those with earnings above the limit. Total discounted income for this group is given by

$$z = y - cm + \{b + p(m - b)\} / (1 + r) \qquad y > m \tag{14}$$

and the second equation in (9) above is now appropriate for the group with $b < y < m$. Calculation of the overall mean and variance by suitable combination of the three groups is obviously more cumbersome than with only two groups, but the basic method proceeds as above. The full formulae are therefore not reproduced here.[1]

---

[1] For the application of similar methods to the analysis of various negative income tax schemes see J. Creedy, 'Negative income taxes and income redistribution', *Oxford Bulletin of Economics and Statistics*, 40, no. 4, 1978.

Contracting out of a flat-rate pension

Define the implicit rate of return on contributions for person i as r_i, which is given by

$$1 + r_i = P(y_i)/C(y_i)$$

Using the relationship between c, b and r (the rate of interest obtained by the fund) for proportional contributions and a flat-rate pension, derived above, it can be seen that

$$(1 + r_i) = (1 + r)\bar{y}/y_i \qquad (15)$$

Thus all individuals with earnings greater than the arithmetic mean obtain a rate of return which is less than the market rate of interest earned by the fund. As explained in chapter 6, to allow such individuals to contract out of the scheme would be unstable, since everyone except the poorest individual would leave the system. To maintain stability it is necessary to reduce the effective rate of interest on savings (the contributions transferred to a private scheme) by individuals who are contracted out. This may be achieved by forcing such individuals to contribute a portion, δc, of their earnings into the state fund, although no state pension is received. The effective interest factor is thereby reduced to $(1 - \delta)(1 + r)$, and there will be some level of earnings y^*, below which there is no incentive to contract out. The value of y^* is the contracting out margin discussed in chapter 6. The relationship between δ and y^*, and the implications for rates of benefits and contributions, may be obtained as follows.

Since by definition $NF(y^*)$ individuals remain in the state scheme, total contributions to the state fund must in this case finance total pension payments of $NbF(y^*)$, rather than Nb. Total contributions are equal to

$$Nc[\int^{y^*}y\,dF(y) + \delta\int_{y^*}y\,dF(y)]$$

which simplifies to

$$Nc\bar{y}\{\delta + (1 - \delta)F_1(y^*)\} \qquad (16)$$

The relationship between $b/\bar{y}$ and the proportional contributions rate c is, as before, obtained by equating total accumulated contributions to total pension payments, giving

$$b/\bar{y} = (1 + r)c\{\delta + (1 - \delta)F_1(y^*)\}/F(y^*) \qquad (17)$$

By equating the effective market rate of return for those contracted out with the rate of return offered to a person with earnings of y^* by the state scheme, the following relationship can be obtained

$$\delta/(1 - \delta) = F(y^*)/(y^*/\bar{y}) - F_1(y^*) \qquad (18)$$

Notice that this does not depend on c, b or r. The results in the second section of chapter 6 are therefore obtained by using (18) to obtain the appropriate value of δ corresponding to a given y^*, and then substituting into (17), with given $(1 + r)c$, to calculate the corresponding value of $b/\bar{y}$.

The transformations between z and y for those above and below y^* can then easily be used, with the method described in the previous section, to calculate the dispersion of net discounted lifetime income.

Partial contracting out of the two-tier pension (no upper limit)

In this system individuals are allowed to contract out of the earnings-related component of the two-tier pension, but receive the flat-rate pension, after contributing δcy rather than cy. As in the previous section those with earnings above the level of y^* contract out, and total contributions are the same as in equation (16). The total amount required to finance the pensions of those remaining in the state scheme is given, after some manipulation, by

$$Nb + Np[\bar{y}\{F_1(y^*) - F_1(b)\} - b\{F(y^*) - F(b)\}] \qquad (19)$$

which may be written as $N\{b + pG(y^*, b)\}$, where $G(y^*, b)$ is the term in square brackets in expression (19). The total contributions, given by the expression in (16), after addition of interest, must then equal total pension payments, given by (19). Thus

$$b + pG(y^*, b) = (1 + r)c\bar{y}\{\delta + (1 - \delta)F_1(y^*)\} \qquad (20)$$

Any set of values satisfying (20) must also satisfy the condition that the implicit rate of return from the state pension for earnings of y^* is equal to the effective market rate of return for those contracted out. This implies that

$$(1 + r)(1 - \delta) = \{b + p(y^* - b)\}/cy^* \qquad (21)$$

Using (20) and (21) to eliminate $(1 + r)c$ gives

$$\frac{\delta}{1 - \delta} = \frac{\{b + pG(y^*, b)\}y^*}{\{b + p(y^* - b)\}\bar{y}} - F_1(y^*) \qquad (22)$$

This corresponds to equation (18), which applied to full contracting out of a flat-rate pension. Equation (22) was therefore used to obtain the results plotted in chart 6.3. Equation (20) was then used to calculate the value of $(1 + r)c$ needed to finance each particular combination of y^*, δ, b and p, for the results shown in chart 6.4.

The population is now divided into three groups, those who receive only the basic pension, those with earnings between b and y^*, and those who contract out. The transformations between z and y for each of these groups provide the within-group means and variances, which can be used for suitable aggregation to obtain the overall dispersion of net discounted life income, shown in chart 6.6.

APPENDIX B

This appendix describes how the pension simulations reported in chapters 4 and 5 were carried out. There are two main elements in the simulation model. First, the process by which individual earnings in each year of working life are generated; and secondly the process by which the age at death is obtained for each individual. Particularly important is the extent to which individuals with relatively higher lifetime earnings tend to live, on average, longer than those with relatively low earnings.

The generation of age-earnings profiles

The basic earnings model from which results presented in chapters 4 and 5 were obtained is in fact over twenty years old, and was first used by Aitchison and Brown.[1] From the point of view of the simulations this model is most conveniently specified as

$$x_{it} = x_{it-1} exp\{f(t) + \varepsilon_{it}\} \qquad (1)$$

where x_{it} is individual i's earnings in year t (t is measured from age 20 when $t = 1$), and $f(t)$ is chosen to generate the profile of median earnings over life. The variable ε_{it} is a stochastic term which governs the nature and extent of individual relative movements within the distribution of contemporaries. If it is assumed that the ε_{it} are independently normally distributed, such that

$$\varepsilon_{it} \quad \text{is} \quad N(o, \sigma_\varepsilon^2) \qquad (2)$$

then proportionate income changes from one period to the next are independent of both relative income and previous proportionate changes. This therefore represents a so-called 'Gibrat' process.[2] It is assumed that

$$f(t) = \alpha(\tau - t) \qquad (3)$$

where α and τ are parameters. The value of τ is the time at which median earnings reach a maximum, and α measures the extent to

[1] *The Lognormal Distribution*, p. 109.
[2] Following the use of this assumption in R. Gibrat, *Les Inégalites Economiques*, Paris, Sirey, 1931.

which the average proportionate increase in earnings declines with advancing age. It is also necessary to make an explicit assumption about the initial distribution of earnings (at age 20 when $t = 1$). It is assumed that earnings are lognormally distributed, so that if $y_{it} = \log_e x_{it}$ then

$$x_{it} \quad \text{is} \quad \Lambda(\mu_1, \sigma_1^2) \quad \text{and} \quad y_{it} \quad \text{is} \quad N(\mu_1, \sigma_1^2) \tag{4}$$

where μ_1 and σ_1^2 are respectively the mean and variance of the natural logarithms of earnings. Equations (1) to (4) can be shown to imply that earnings in each age group are lognormally distributed, that the mean of the logarithms of earnings is a quadratic function of time and that the variance of the logarithms of earnings increases linearly with time. Thus

$$x_t \quad \text{is} \quad \Lambda\left(x_t \mid \mu_1 + \alpha\tau t - \frac{\alpha}{2}t^2, \sigma_1^2 + \sigma_\varepsilon^2 t\right) \tag{5}$$

It is then necessary to obtain appropriate values for the five parameters included in equation (5).

Parameter values

The parameter values were estimated using data provided by the Department of Health and Social Security, which were originally compiled in order to operate the National Insurance and Graduated Pension schemes. It is important to stress that the author has not had access to the original data source and there is no possibility of identifying any individual; complete anyonymity has been maintained throughout.

Information about the annual earnings (from all sources as defined for income tax purposes) is available for the years 1963, 1968, 1971-2-3 for cohorts born in 1943 and 1923; and for the years 1963, 1966, 1970-1-2 -3 for the cohort born in 1933. Individuals who paid less than 48 class 1 National Insurance contributions in any of the relevant years were excluded from the samples. These data were used to obtain the mean and variance of the logarithms of earnings for each year and cohort, and all values of μ_t were adjusted to 1973 prices using a consumer price index. These adjusted values of μ_t are shown in chart B1, which clearly indicates the phenomenon of overtaking discussed in chapter 4. After suitable combination of the profiles for each cohort, on the assumption that cohort 1943 will experience similar *rates* of growth to cohorts 1933 and 1923 at comparable ages, the following estimates were obtained

$$x_t \quad \text{is} \quad \Lambda(x_t \mid 6{\cdot}95 + 0{\cdot}0876t - 0{\cdot}0013t^2, 0{\cdot}066 + 0{\cdot}004t) \tag{6}$$

These values apply to a synthetic cohort profile which is appropriate only for the cohort born in 1943.[1]

---

[1] For further discussion of the data and method used to obtain parameter estimates, see Creedy and Hart, 'Age and the distribution of earnings'.

The simulated profiles

The object is to obtain a matrix $X = \{x_{it}\}$ of earnings over $t = 1, \ldots, T$ periods for $i = 1, \ldots, N$ individuals. First, it is necessary to generate the earnings of each individual in the sample for the case where $t = 1$ (that is, for age 20 years). From (2) it is clear that $(y_{i1} - \mu_1)/\sigma_1$ is distributed as an $N(0, 1)$ variable. Thus using the values of μ_1 and σ_1^2 from (6) of 6·95 and 0·066 respectively, an appropriate value of y_{i1} can be obtained as $\mu_1 + \sigma_1 u_{i1}$, where u_{i1} is a random standard Normal variable. Then y_{i1} is equal to $exp(y_{i1})$. This can be repeated for all individuals to obtain a simulated distribution of initial earnings.

The first stage is therefore actually to obtain, using a suitable method for the generation of random Normal deviates, a matrix $u = \{u_{it}\}$ for $t = 1, \ldots, T$ and $i = 1, \ldots, N$. Having obtained the initial distribution of earnings, a complete profile from $t = 2, \ldots, T$ can then be obtained recursively using equation (1). The value of ε_{it} is obtained using (2) as $\varepsilon_{it} = \sigma_\varepsilon u_{it}$, and that of $f(t)$ by appropriate substitution into (3). These values can then be directly substituted into (1).

The simulations were carried out for $t = 1, \ldots, 45$ periods, but the difficult problem of deciding on the size of simulated sample was settled after a number of sensitivity analyses using progressively larger values of N. The values of μ_t and σ_t^2 obtained from the simulations were sufficiently stable for a sample size of $N = 300$ individuals.

Alternative specifications of mobility

Although equation (6) provides a good description of the profiles of μ_t and σ_t^2, it is important to examine the sensitivity of the results to alternative specifications of the process of year to year changes in earnings. It is possible to allow for current changes to be dependent on past changes, and for Galtonian Regression towards the mean,[1] using the following system of equations.

$$x_{it} = \left(\frac{x_{i, t-1}}{m_{t-1}}\right)^\beta \exp(\mu_t + \varepsilon_{it}) \tag{7}$$

where
$$m_t = \exp(\mu_t) \quad \text{and} \quad \mu_t = \mu_{t-1} + f(t) \tag{8}$$

$$\varepsilon_{it} = \gamma \varepsilon_{i, t-1} + \xi_{it} \tag{9}$$

with
$$\xi_{it} \quad \text{as} \quad N(0, \sigma_\xi^2) \tag{10}$$

---

[1] 'Galtonian Regression' refers to the extent to which individuals with higher than average earnings experience (on average) relatively lower percentage increases in earnings. The various specifications of mobility are examined in J. Creedy, 'Income changes over the life cycle', *Oxford Economic Papers*, vol. 26, November 1974.

Chart B.1. *Variation in mean log-earnings with age*

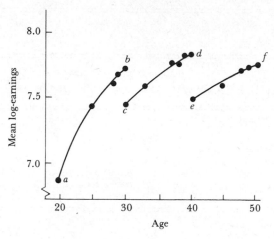

KEY
ab = cohort 1943
cd = cohort 1933
ef = cohort 1923

This alternative specification therefore requires the additional parameters β, σ_{ξ}^2 and γ, although σ_{ε}^2 is no longer needed. In order to obtain the initial distribution, the condition that $\varepsilon_{i1} = \xi_{i1}$ is also used. For $t = 2$, ..., T a similar process to that used earlier is employed. Of particular interest here is the variation in the x_{it}'s which results from the use of different specifications, so that in order to reduce the extent of independent variation in the results it was decided to use the same set of u_{it}'s for each of the simulated samples.

Some characteristics of the age-earnings profiles which result from different specifications are given in tables B.1 and B.2. Before examining the consequences for contribution and benefits it is first necessary to consider the determination of the length of retirement.

Differential mortality

As mentioned in chapter 4, the age at death for each individual is also obtained using a stochastic relationship. The death rate depends partly on the individual's relative position in the distribution of annual average lifetime earnings, and partly on stochastic or chance factors which are unrelated to earnings. Only the costs and benefits of those who survive to pension age are considered, so that there are no deaths until age 65 years. The formula reflects the assumption that those with relatively

Table B.1. *Values of μ_t at selected ages: all samples*

Age	25	30	35	40	45	50	55	60	65
μ_t	7·29	7·60	7·88	8·07	8·20	8·27	8·28	8·22	8·10

Table B.2. *Values of σ_t^2 at selected ages: alternative samples*

Sample no.	Parameter values				Value of σ_t^2								
	σ_ε^2	σ_ξ^2	γ	β	25	30	35	40	45	50	55	60	65
1	0·004		0	1	0·083	0·106	0·128	0·147	0·172	0·197	0·252	0·285	0·304
2	—	0·008	−0·2	1	0·069	0·102	0·130	0·157	0·195	0·227	0·302	0·342	0·370
3	—	0·002	+0·2	1	0·119	0·136	0·154	0·169	0·187	0·208	0·251	0·282	0·296
4	0·015	—	0	0·95	0·092	0·124	0·137	0·140	0·162	0·171	0·213	0·191	0·173

Note: Sample size (all samples) = 300

high lifetime earnings tend to live longer than average, and vice versa.[1] Age at death is obtained from

$$d_i = \bar{d} + \theta \log (x_i/x_g) + u_i \tag{11}$$

where d_i = number of years person i survives after retirement

$\bar{d}$ = average of d_i's

x_i = person i's annual average earnings

x_g = geometric mean value of the x_i's

u_i = random variable distributed as $N(0, \sigma_u^2)$

The value of $\bar{d}$ is set at 12 years, since the expectation of life for males who survive to age 65 is 77 years. The values of x_i and x_g are of course obtained directly from the earnings simulations. It is therefore necessary to make specific assumptions about the values of θ and σ_u^2. An important criterion in setting these values is that the implied survival curve should approximate the actual curve for males in Great Britain. Now from equation (11) where $V(\log x_i) = \sigma_x^2$:

$$E(d_i) = \bar{d} \quad \text{and} \quad V(d_i) = \theta^2\sigma_x^2 + \sigma_u^2 \tag{12}$$

If, furthermore, x_i is assumed to be lognormally distributed, then

$$d_i \quad \text{is} \quad N(\bar{d}, \theta^2\sigma_x^2 + \sigma_u^2)$$

[1] It has been mentioned in chapter 3 that appropriate data do not exist for Great Britain. The same is true of the United States, but an extensive study is by E. M. Kitagawa and P. H. Hauser, *Differential Mortality in the USA. A Study in Socioeconomic Epidemiology*, Cambridge Mass., Harvard University Press, 1973.

Table B.3. *Alternative samples*

Sample no.	Measure of earnings	Arithmetic mean £s
2	Final year	3942
	Average lifetime	3335
	Average best 20 years	4525
3	Final year	3871
	Average lifetime	3357
	Average best 20 years	4436
4	Final year	3588
	Average lifetime	3214
	Average best 20 years	4407

and the proportion who survive until at least d years after retirement, $s(d)$ say, is given by

$$s(d) = 1 - N\{(d - \overline{d})(\theta^2\sigma_x^2 + \sigma_u^2)^{-\frac{1}{2}}\,|\,0, 1\} \tag{13}$$

equation (13) can then be used to calculate a survival curve for alternative values of θ and σ_u^2. Values of 2 and 36 for θ and σ_u^2 respectively were found to produce a survival curve which compares closely with that for males in Great Britain. The implications for differential mortality of the value of θ can be seen as follows. For individuals whose earnings arc 20 per cent of the geometric mean, the expectation of life at 65 years is reduced by just over three years. Much higher earnings have little additional effect, however, since those with earnings which are twice the mean have their expectation of life at 65 increased by just over one year.

Alternative results

Arithmetic means of some alternative distributions of earnings, using samples 2, 3 and 4, are given in table B.3; the sample numbers refer to those in table B.2. These results may be compared with those presented in chapter 4 for the basic model (sample 1). It can be seen that the main results are not sensitive to the assumptions of Gibrat and Markov.[1]

---

[1] Further comparisons between alternative models are given in J. Creedy, 'The new government pension scheme: a simulation analysis', *Oxford Bulletin of Economics and Statistics*, 42, no. 1, 1980.

APPENDIX C

This appendix examines some implications of integrating National Insurance contributions and the income tax system. These implications are not immediately clear since the two systems are based on very different sets of principles, although it is sometimes suggested that integration would require a new rate of income tax equal to the sum of the former two rates (of taxes and of contributions). In fact the appropriate rate in an integrated system depends crucially on how the objectives of the system are framed; in particular whether it is desired to maintain total revenue at a constant level, or whether it is required to achieve a specified distribution of post-tax income. The first of these approaches is considered below.

Total revenue

Consider first the total revenue which would be raised from an income tax system which has a single marginal tax rate of t on taxable income, and where the latter is calculated as income *above* a specified level of allowances. If the fixed level of allowances is denoted by a, and gross income by y, then the tax schedule $T(y)$ is given by

$$T(y) = 0 \qquad y \leq a$$
$$\qquad = t(y - a) \qquad y > a \tag{1}$$

The total tax revenue *per capita* clearly depends on the proportion of people with incomes above a, $1 - F(a)$, and on the amount of their total income which is above a and liable for taxation. The total income exempt from taxation is $N\{1 - F(a)\}a$, where N is the total number of people. This must be subtracted from the total income of taxpayers, $N\bar{y}\{1 - F_1(a)\}$, to give the total income liable for tax

$$N[\bar{y}\{1 - F_1(a)\} - a\{1 - F(a)\}] \tag{2}$$

After dividing by N and multiplying by the tax rate t, the total tax revenue *per capita*, R_t, is given as

$$R_t = t\bar{y}\{1 - h(a)\} \tag{3}$$

$$\text{with} \quad h(a) = F_1(a) + a\{1 - F(a)\}/\bar{y} \tag{4}$$

If there were no allowances then the tax revenue per person would be $t\bar{y}$, so that $h(a)$ measures the effect of such allowances. It should be noted that the same function was used in appendix A, where it was also necessary to divide the population into several components according to individuals' incomes.

Consider next the system of National Insurance contributions. The main characteristics of this system, which make it so different from the income tax system, are that contributions are proportional to *gross* income, but are not levied on incomes below a lower limit, y_0 say, and above an upper limit, m say.[1] The marginal contributions rate is therefore extremely high at the lower limit, and zero at and above the upper limit. The contributions schedule $C(y)$, can be written as

$$\begin{aligned} C(y) &= 0 & y < y_0 \\ &= cy & y_0 \leq y \leq m \\ &= cm & y > m \end{aligned} \tag{5}$$

Total National Insurance contributions per head, R_c, are therefore given by

$$\begin{aligned} R_c &= \int C(y)\,dF(y) \\ &= \int_{y_0}^{m} y\,dF(y) + cm \int_{m} dF(y) \end{aligned} \tag{6}$$

Equation (6) can then be simplified in the same way as equation (2), so that some manipulation gives

$$R_c = c\bar{y}\{h(m) - F_1(y_0)\} \tag{7}$$

A crucial characteristic of the present British system which combines National Insurance contributions and income taxation is that insurance contributions are *not* deducted from income before obtaining the value of taxable income. Since the distribution of gross income, y, is assumed to be exogenous (that is, not affected by the tax structure), the two systems are therefore independent. The total revenue per head is simply the sum of (3) and (7).

The tax rate, t', required for an integrated system to provide the same

---

[1] In fact contributions are voluntary for those with earnings below y_0, in order to maintain eligibility for National Insurance benefits. In much of the discussion of pensions in this book it was assumed that individuals were eligible for full benefits, so that the lower earnings limit to contributions was often ignored.

total revenue as the combined insurance and tax system (with tax rate t) is therefore obtained by solving for t' from the expression

$$R_{t'} = R_t + R_c$$

where $R_{t'}$ is obtained from equation (3) after substituting t' for t. Thus

$$t' = t + c\{h(m) - F_{\scriptscriptstyle 1}(y_0)\}/\{1 - h(a)\} \tag{9}$$

A numerical example

In order to provide an indication of the order of magnitude involved it is necessary to specify the distribution function, $F(y)$, and to use a functional form which has a convenient first moment distribution $F_{\scriptscriptstyle 1}(y)$. The obvious case here, as in appendix A, is the lognormal distribution, for which

$$F(y) = \Lambda(y \mid \mu, \sigma^2) \quad \text{and} \quad F_{\scriptscriptstyle 1}(y) = \Lambda(\mu + \sigma^2, \sigma^2) \tag{10}$$

where μ and σ^2 are respectively the mean and variance of the logarithms of income. Suitable parameter values, as in appendix A, are $\mu = 8\cdot2$ and $\sigma^2 = 0\cdot2$, which imply an arithmetic mean income of £5431 and a coefficient of variation of $0\cdot471$. If the upper limit, m, is equal to £8000 (so that $m/\bar{y} = 1\cdot473$) then $F(m) = 0\cdot862$, $F_{\scriptscriptstyle 1}(m) = 0\cdot740$, and $h(m) = 0\cdot943$. If $y_0 = $ £1400 (so that $y_0/\bar{y} = 0\cdot257$) then $F(y_0) = 0\cdot002$ and $F_{\scriptscriptstyle 1}(y_0) = 0\cdot001$. Finally, suppose that $a = $ £1600, for which $1 - h(a) = 0\cdot705$.

Now if the rate of insurance contributions is $0\cdot15$ the tax rate t' required to raise the same total revenue as the combined system is given by

$$t' = t + (0\cdot15)(0\cdot942)/(0\cdot705)$$

$$= t + 0\cdot200$$

Thus, the single tax rate in the integrated system would have to be larger than the sum of the two separate rates. The addition would be 5 percentage points (or one third) on the postulated insurance rate of $0\cdot15$.[1] The burden of taxation in the two systems is of course quite different.[2]

---

[1] This result contrasts with the discussion in Meade *et al*, *The Structure and Reform of Direct Taxation*, pp. 374–5, which suggests that the rate would be approximately equal to the sum of the two separate rates.

[2] For further discussion of these issues see J. Creedy, 'Taxation and National Insurance contributions in Britain', *Journal of Public Economics*, *15*, 1981, and J. Creedy, 'The changing burden of National Insurance contributions and income taxation in Britain', *Scottish Journal of Political Economy*, *29*, no. 2, 1982.

INDEX

RECENT PUBLICATIONS OF THE
NATIONAL INSTITUTE OF ECONOMIC
AND SOCIAL RESEARCH

published by
THE CAMBRIDGE UNIVERSITY PRESS

ECONOMIC AND SOCIAL STUDIES

XXVI   *Urban Development in Britain: Standards, Costs and Resources, 1964–2004*
By P. A. STONE. Vol. I: *Population Trends and Housing.* 1970. pp. 436. £17·75 net.

XXVII   *The Framework of Regional Economics in the United Kingdom*
By A. J. BROWN. 1972. pp. 372. £20·25 net.

XXVIII   *The Structure, Size and Costs of Urban Settlements*
By P. A. STONE. 1973. pp. 304. £14·50 net.

XXIX   *The Diffusion of New Industrial Processes: An International Study*
Edited by L. NABSETH and G. F. RAY. 1974. pp. 346. £18·25 net.

XXXI   *British Economic Policy 1960–74*
Edited by F. T. BLACKABY. 1978. pp. 710. £32·50 net.

XXXII   *Industrialisation and the Basis for Trade*
By R. A. BATCHELOR, R. L. MAJOR and A. D. MORGAN. 1980. pp. 380. £19·75 net.

XXXIII   *Productivity and Industrial Structure*
By S. J. PRAIS. 1981. pp. 401. £20·00 net.

OCCASIONAL PAPERS

XXV   *The Analysis and Forecasting of the British Economy*
By M. J. C. SURREY. 1971. pp. 120. £7·50 net.

XXVI   *Mergers and Concentration in British Industry*
By P. E. HART, M. A. UTTON and G. WALSHE. 1973. pp. 190. £9·95 net.

XXVII   *Recent Trends in Monopoly in Great Britain*
By G. WALSHE. 1974. pp. 156. £9·25 net.

XXVIII   *Cyclical Indicators for the Postwar British Economy*
By D. J. O'DEA. 1975. pp. 184. £10·95 net.

XXIX   *Poverty and Progress in Britain, 1953–73*
By G. C. FIEGEHEN, P. S. LANSLEY and A. D. SMITH. 1977. pp. 192. £11·50 net.

XXX   *The Innovation Process in the Energy Industries*
By G. F. RAY and L. UHLMANN. 1979. pp. 132. £8·50 net.

XXXI   *Diversification and Competition*
By M. A. UTTON. 1979. pp. 124. £9·75 net.

XXXII   *Concentration in British Industry, 1935–75*
By P. E. HART and R. CLARKE. 1980. pp. 178. £11·25 net.

NIESR STUDENTS' EDITION

1   *Growth and Trade* (abridged from *Industrial Growth and World Trade*)
By A. MAIZELS. 1970. pp. 312. £5·75 net.

2   *The Antitrust Laws of the U.S.A.* (3rd edition, unabridged)
By A. D. NEALE and D. G. GOYDER. 1980. pp. 544. £9·95 net.

4   *British Economic Policy 1960–74: Demand Management* (an abridged version of *British Economic Policy 1960–74*)
Edited by F. T. BLACKABY. 1979. pp. 472. £8·95 net.

5   *The Evolution of Giant Firms in Britain* (2nd impression with a new preface)
By S. J. PRAIS. 1981. pp. 344. £7·50 net.

REGIONAL PAPERS

1 *The Anatomy of Regional Activity Rates* by JOHN BOWERS, and *Regional Social Accounts for the United Kingdom* by V. H. WOODWARD. 1970. pp. 192. £6·75 net.

2 *Regional Unemployment Differences in Great Britain* by P. C. CHESHIRE, and *Interregional Migration Models and their Application to Great Britain* by R. WEEDEN. 1973. pp. 118. £6·75 net.

3 *Unemployment, Vacancies and the Rate of Change of Earnings: A Regional Analysis* by A. E. WEBB, and *Regional Rates of Employment Growth: An Analysis of Variance Treatment* by R. WEEDEN. 1974. pp. 114. £6·75 net.

THE NATIONAL INSTITUTE OF ECONOMIC AND SOCIAL RESEARCH

publishes regularly

THE NATIONAL INSTITUTE ECONOMIC REVIEW

A quarterly analysis of the general economic situation in the United Kingdom and the world overseas, with forecasts eighteen months ahead. The last issue each year contains an assessment of medium-term prospects. There are also in most issues special articles on subjects of interest to acadmic and business economists.

Annual subscriptions, £25·00 (home), and £35·00 (abroad), also single issues for the current year, £7·00 (home) and £10·00 (abroad), are available directly from NIESR, 2 Dean Trench Street, Smith Square, London, SWIP 3HE.

Subscriptions at the special reduced price of £10·00 p.a. are available to students in the United Kingdom and Irish Republic on application to the Secretary of the Institute.

Back numbers and reprints of issues which have gone out of stock are distributed by Wm. Dawson and Sons Ltd., Cannon House, Park Farm Road, Folkestone. Microfiche copies for the years 1959–80 are available from EP Microform Ltd, Bradford Road, East Ardsley, Wakefield, Yorks.

Published by
HEINEMANN EDUCATIONAL BOOKS

AN INCOMES POLICY FOR BRITAIN
Edited by FRANK BLACKABY. 1972. pp. 260. £5·95 net.

THE UNITED KINGDOM ECONOMY
by the NIESR. 4th edn, 1979. pp. 128. £1·80 net.

DEMAND MANAGEMENT
Edited by MICHAEL POSNER. 1978. pp. 256. £5·50 (paperback) net.

DE-INDUSTRIALISATION
Edited by FRANK BLACKABY. 1979. pp. 282. £9·50 (hardback), £6·50 (paperback) net.

BRITAIN'S TRADE AND EXCHANGE-RATE POLICY
Edited by ROBIN MAJOR. 1979. pp. 240. £12·50 (hardback), £6·50 (paperback) net.

BRITAIN IN EUROPE
Edited by WILLIAM WALLACE. 1980. pp.224. £10·50 (hardback), £4·95 (paperback) net.

THE FUTURE OF PAY BARGAINING
Edited by FRANK BLACKABY. 1980. pp. 246. £13·50 (hardback), £6·50 (paperback) net.

INDUSTRIAL POLICY AND INNOVATION
Edited by CHARLES CARTER. 1981. pp. 241. £14·50 (hardback), £6·50 (paperback) net.